COMMISSION OF THE EUROPEAN COMMUNITIES

Loan Guarantees for Large Infrastructure Projects: the issues and possible lessons for a European facility

Cataloguing data can be found at the end of this publication.

Luxembourg: Office for Official Publications of the European Communities, 1993

ISBN 92-826-5675-6

Printed in France

Loan Guarantees for Large Infrastructure Projects: the issues and possible lessons for a European facility

by

Stephany Griffith-Jones

Dr. Stephany Griffith-Jones is a Fellow at the Institute of Development Studies, University of Sussex. Previously she has worked at Barclays Bank International UK, and the Central Bank of Chile.

Dr. Griffith-Jones has acted as senior consultant to many international agencies, including the EEC, the World Bank, the Inter-American Development Bank, UNICEF, UNCTAD and others. She has also acted as consultant to several governments, including the British and the new Chilean government.

Dr. Griffith-Jones has published very widely in the fields of international finance and macro-economic policy. Her two most recent articles are: "Conversion of Official Bilateral Debt" published in Proceedings of World Bank Annual Conference on Development Economics 1992, World Bank, and "The Return of Latin America to Private Capital Markets" in Fragile Finance, published by FONDAD, Netherlands.

*   *
*

ACKNOWLEDGEMENTS

This publication is based on a study which was commissioned by the Commission of the European Communities' Directorate General XXII. Part of it was presented at a workshop in Brussels on "Guarantees for Funding Large Infrastructure Projects Inside the European Community", held on 11 and 12 June 1992.

I am particularly grateful to David McGlue and Margarida da Gama Santos of the European Commission for their challenging comments and questions of substance throughout the course of my research; for their specific advice on European Community financing of major infrastructure projects both past and present; and for their considerable help, with the support of Thomas Angelius, in revising and updating the text for publication.

I also wish to thank many people who have given their time and knowledge, especially F. Vibert, R. Mathrani, P. Mistry, S. Hudson, G. Haley, A. Watkins, J. Taylor, L. Hollywood, N. Allington and I. Shihata. I am also grateful to several staff members of the European Investment Bank, including M. Deleau, A. Steinherr, H. Kuhrt, T. Barrett, and A. Gilibert for their useful insights. Last but certainly not least, considerable thanks are due to Tracie Gunn of the Institute for Development Studies and Dörthe Ohm of the European Commission for their very efficient production and revision of a long and complex manuscript.

CONTENTS

BOXES

TABLES

EXECUTIVE SUMMARY AND RECOMMENDATIONS

This report supports the case for the creation at European Community level of a guarantee facility for large infrastructure projects and indicates some guidelines for such a facility, drawn from international experience.

The core of the business of such a facility would be the provision of guarantees on financing by the private sector of investment projects in trans-European networks (eg. high-speed train connections and other transport infrastructures, telecommunication systems and energy transmission lines forming parts of networks linking together several member states) throughout the Community.

The report does not examine the arguments for similar support for small- and medium-sized enterprises.

THE RATIONALE

The recommendations are based first of all on an analysis of the needs and current limitations of the market in financing large infrastructure projects and of the types of risk which such projects face.

The Market Situation

The retreat of the public sector. Internationally governments and private actors are increasingly collaborating in mixed private/public sector operations to fund and run large infrastructure projects. There has been a growing recourse to different forms of private (co)financing since most governments face budget constraints and wish to enlarge the role of the private sector.

The role of the public sector is thus changing - more rapidly in some countries than in other - from responsibility for all aspects of infrastructure projects to that more simply for the initiation of projects, taking care of the public interest, and setting the framework within which contractors, financiers and other parties from the private sector build, own and operate the infrastructure needed. This may take place through the so-called BOT (Build-Operate-Transfer) model of project financing under which private businesses sign a concession contract with the government under which they are awarded the right to build, own and operate the infrastructure project on a non-recourse or limited recourse basis, limiting the government's role to regulator and promoter. The BOT model uses a variety of sources of finance relying both on debt and equity capital. When the project fails to forecast an adequate return, an element of grant aid may be needed to complete the equity component (the "equity gap") in order to make it attractive to private sector finance.

Constraints on the volume of bank lending. Coinciding with increased reliance on private funds for infrastructure the banking industry's capacity to provide such funding is stagnating or may even be contracting. This is due to both cyclical factors (eg. the current recession and deteriorating quality of many of the banking sector's assets) as well as structural reasons (eg. capital adequacy requirements and restrictions on large exposures derived from BIS and EC rules). These factors may bear particularly heavily on long-term projects.

Market failures. The picture is further complicated by other market failures:

- *the time-horizon of bankers.* Often infrastructure projects need financing for periods up to 25-30 years while the private market normally will only provide loans with significantly shorter maturities.

- *less developed capital markets in some member states.* In for instance Greece and Portugal it may well be even more difficult than elsewhere to obtain at a competitive interest rate the large loans and especially the long maturities needed.

- *the absence of natural private ownership for infrastructure investments.* Since this kind of project has been dealt with in the past by the public sector there is a lack of private sector experience in ownership/management of large infrastructure projects. This can lead to a particularly cautious attitude towards this kind of project on the part of commercial banks.

x

- *externalities*. Traditional public sector decisions have taken into account indirect economic costs and benefits. Private investors only consider direct costs and revenues. They would not, for instance, include in their evaluations the benefits for the surrounding economy of a new motorway, since they focus simply on the profitability of the project itself.

The risks

Special uncertainties. Due to the distinctive nature of large infrastructure projects potential investors face risks that differ from those of typical productive investments.

The risk assessment of large infrastructure projects has to be dealt with in a particularly rigorous way for several reasons:

- a combination of high capital costs and low operating costs implies that financing costs are a very large proportion of the total

- long construction periods are most often combined with slow build-up of revenue

- the project's cash-flow is the crucial element in the return to equity investors and in the security of lenders (in the absence of public guarantees).

A typical infrastructure project has at least three clearly distinct phases, in which different risks need to be clearly identified.

First, there is the **promotion and preparation stage**. Though substantial costs can be incurred in this stage - often over an extended period - there is no certainty that at the end of the period the concession will be won or even that the investment will take place. In the case of international projects these risks may often be higher due to the involvement of several countries.

Second, there is a **high risk construction phase**. In this stage a number of risks of both political and commercial nature can arise.

The *construction and completion risk* primarily consists of risks of delays in commencing construction (planning permissions, environmental impact studies with associated public enquiries), cost overruns and delays arising from force majeure. There is a small private insurance market willing to insure against certain specific risks (eg. technical non-performance and contractor or supplier lateness) but most commercial lenders would be unwilling to assume the remaining risk.

Third, there is a **relatively lower risk operating phase**. Here the main risks are:

- *factors affecting operating returns* eg. technical risk (facility does not perform at rated levels), market risk (shortfall in demand compared with market forecasts) and regulatory risk (the government might change certain rules eg. on safety)

- risks arising from *public sector purchases of outputs or suppliers of inputs*

- risks arising from possible *changes in public transport policies* that might affect for example the level of traffic

- *externalities* that might adversely affect costs (eg. payment to compensate a negative environmental effect).

The risks are often magnified in the case of transnational projects such as intra-EC projects which pose problems of interconnections and interoperability (see Annex) of systems and where different traditions of financing and regulation by governments apply in different countries.

LOAN GUARANTEE FACILITIES: SOME INTERNATIONAL EXPERIENCE

A review of international experience demonstrates how loan guarantee mechanisms have been developed to meet some of the problems discussed above. It serves to highlight both the advantages of guarantee mechanisms and some of the pitfalls to avoid.

The World Bank. In 1983 the World Bank, which sought to extend credit enhancement to commercial lenders, created a co-financing programme known as the *B-Loan programme* which included an element of guarantees aimed in particular at overcoming the reluctance of banks to lend for very long terms. Through this programme the World Bank could participate in a commercial bank loans by several mechanisms, for examply by guaranteeing later maturities up to 25% of the total principal amount of the loan.

Prospective lenders viewed the narrow definition of bank support (late maturities) as too limited; also the programme was geared to a to narrow section of the "potential market" (public sector borrowing in the syndicated loan market).

As a result of these problems and of the need to adapt to changing patterns of financial flows to developing countries, *ECO* (Expanded Co-financing Operations) was introduced in 1989. ECO allows the World Bank to extend guarantees to commercial loans and bond issues. The support can be adapted to meet borrower needs and market requirements, but the private sector has to bear all commercial risks. The guiding principle for the Bank is to use the minimum support necessary to mobilize the needed resources in a manner that minimises the risk to the World Bank itself.

On the other hand, the extended "preferred creditor status" of IFC of the World Bank Group has attracted a large number of banks since its legal structure seems more attractive than that of ECO. One key factor is that banks jointly providing finance with IFC for a loan are not required to make provisions for the loans since the IFC acts as the sole lender of record and administrator.

MIGA (Multilateral Investment Guarantee Agency) was established in 1988 as a part of the World Bank Group to encourage the flow of private foreign investment to promote development in member states. MIGA (mainly) insures investments made by foreign investors against losses caused by political risks defined as losses in currency transfer, losses by expropriation, losses by war or civil disturbance and losses from breach of contract.

MIGA has been criticized for having too many rules in its Convention and for lacking agility in operational procedures, but it has interesting organisational features that may be relevant to the establishment of a Community facility (eg. provisions on gearing, risk and price differentiation).

The US private guarantee market offers highly developed forms of credit enhancement. A particularly important element is the upgrading of bond ratings. Under this system the issuer or the underwriter of a security purchases a financial guarantee to insure the timely payment of principal and interest in the event of the issuer's default. As a result, the bond's rating is enhanced - typically to AAA - thereby lowering the issuer's borrowing costs.

The US private guarantee market is very well developed and is often used to guarantee public municipal bonds that are used to fund infrastructure projects. An interesting feature of the system is that upgrading bond ratings makes them a feasible alternative to bank loans. This gives an opportunity for institutional investors as well as small investors to participate in the financing of infrastructures. Especially small investors might prefer the security of bonds to possible larger yields from other less stable investments. The participation in financing might in turn introduce a degree of cooperation between these investors and the banking sector. Another advantage is that the enhancement of credit gives the possibility of matching timeframes between investor and the project to be financed. A drawback of the American system is the limited competition due to the fact that the financial guarantees are typically sold by bank consortia. In addition to the rather uniform municipal bond insurance market there is also a far more complex and diverse corporate financial guarantee market.

Experience from the US market indicates that often the main economic value to the debt issuer is not the assumption of default risk, but assurance of improved market liquidity, lower borrowing costs, collateral monitoring services or avoidance of regulations affecting issuers or purchasers of debt securities. Furthermore the banks are also using such financing to manage their balance sheets.

All in all the American system offers an interesting way of widening the possible sources of financing. In Europe the financial guarantee industry is only just starting and is far smaller in scale than in the US. A Community facility could help develop this market benefitting from the US experience.

From the above review conducted of the loan guarantee mechanisms, conclusions of interest for a future loan guarantee facility can be summarized in the following terms.

On the negative side:

(a) constraints on ECO operations and MIGA instruments as a result of excessive regulation in statutes and operational rules;

(b) regulatory treatment of co-financing operations of the World Bank with commercial banks which offered conditions inferior to the operations funded **solely** by multilateral financial institutions (20% risk-weighting for capital adequacy purposes under BIS rules); and

(c) the difficulty for the World Bank itself in offering on its own balance-sheet an attractive guarantee product to the private sector while at the same time meeting the strict requirements of the rating agencies in granting triple A rating

are aspects that made those schemes less successful and demanded.

On the positive side:

(a) The flexibility of the gearing ratio provision, as well as risk and price differentiation procedures of MIGA;

(b) the fact that MIGA and IFC operations enjoy favourable treatment with respect to BIS capital adequacy ratio requirements in guaranteeing and co-financing with commercial banks;

(c) MIGA's membership of both host and lender/investor countries which facilitates the identification of viable project proposals; and

(d) the role of US financial guarantees of municipal bonds in upgrading bond ratings to triple A, thus lowering borrowing costs to issuers and significantly expanding the individual investor as well as institutional investor markets

are points which may be worth emulating.

Project Case studies. International case experience was examined, ranging from projects with no explicit government guarantees where the investors were prepared to rely on the security provided by prospective revenues and assets, to cases with a fairly large amount of government direct support and guarantees.

In the first category of projects are the Channel Tunnel and four California projects (Caltrans) where there are no explicit government guarantees. However, in the Channel Tunnel governments were active in other ways to support private finance (e.g., French government investment in ancillary connection with the Tunnel) and there was multilateral support through EIB loans. In the California projects case, authorisations by the state were granted for the use of other facilities which will bring in future additional profitability, thus enhancing the private sector return from these projects.

In the second category are the Sydney Harbour Tunnel and the Bilbao Behobia motorway projects. The Sydney Harbour Tunnel enjoyed a fairly large amount of government direct support in subsidies and guarantees, including guarantees on commercial risk. The Bilbao Behobia motorway received more limited government support, mainly foreign exchange risk.

An interesting intermediate project is the Hub River in Pakistan which received public guarantees provided by the World Bank and JEXIM specifically targeted at fuel supply and at off-take of energy, both managed by state companies. They also cover broader political risk relevant only to developing and Eastern European countries and related to the availability of foreign exchange.

RECOMMENDATIONS

The Maastricht Intergovernmental Conference gave a clear Community backing to trans-European networks and underlined the importance of guarantees as one way of attracting private capital.

The creation of a specific loan guarantee facility at Community level would help to meet the market needs analyzed. It could also be an effective and efficient way to use Community resources, providing important leverage in relation to the capital provided from the Community budget.

The experience of other organisations and schemes suggests some guidelines to maximize benefits and minimize problems.

Viable projects. The facility, while taking into account some strictly defined externalities should only guarantee projects that are appraised to be both technically and economically viable.

Exclusion of certain risks. The facility should not be an all purpose mechanism but should aim at adding value to the guarantee market and avoiding competition with the commercial banks. The facility should exclude certain types of risk such as cost and time overruns in the construction phase as well as some purely commercial risks (eg. technical risks or shortfalls in demand compared with market forecasts) thereby avoiding problems with moral hazard and adverse selection.

The reasons why the market may fail to provide financing for such projects (long maturities and transnational character of the project) as well as the complexities of putting together financial packages of such dimensions should be a guide to the areas of guarantee operations and type of risks to be covered.

Differentiated pricing. It is important that the price of guarantees reflects the specific risk(s) to be insured against. One might also consider the scope for contractual arrangements that provide for **upside** benefits to the facility as well as coverage of **downside** risks. Allowing the facility potentially to share in the benefits if the projects perform better than expected would have the advantage that fees and/or premia charged could be lower.

Diversification of portfolio. A precise risk identification together with an amount of relatively low risk operations would imply both diversification of risk throughout the portfolio and increase the financial security of the new instrument itself.

Avoid too many rules. In spite of the need for exclusion of certain risks it is important to ensure the facility's operationability and flexibility by not loading statutes and operational rules with too many pre-determined circumstances of guarantee use but leaving as many of those decisions as possible to the management. The Statutes should outline the objectives of financial viability, the principle of differentiated pricing and define appropriate gearing ratios.

Separate Institutional set-up. The question of whether the facility would be better established as a separate institution or, for example, as a department of the Community's investment bank, the EIB, is related to the perceived risks of the guarantees to be undertaken. The risks of the facility's operations differ in various ways from the risks of normal EIB operations and its establishment within the Bank might endanger the EIB's AAA rating, this being even more so if external market financial institutions should participate as shareholders in the facility. Therefore, there is a strong case for a separate institutional set-up.

A certain amount of capital and a flexible gearing ratio. In order to make the fund viable it is necessary that the investors subscribe and also pay in a certain amount of capital that would ensure the fund's liquidity and allow for a substantial contribution to the funding of large infrastructure projects.

As far as the gearing ratio is concerned flexibility should be ensured at the outset. An interesting formula might be the one employed by MIGA. The initial gearing ratio established in MIGA's convention (150%) may be raised (to 500%) if MIGA's Council so decides. Such a decision-making rule (though not the specific MIGA ratios) could be followed.

Issues deserving further study:

While the study was conducted, several areas emerged deserving further investigation. Among them, the following may be highlighted:

- Whether such an institution might have any useful role to play at the stage of the project conception and tendering (the development phase of the BOT model) or whether other Community or national sources may be better suited.

- Specific cases and possible approaches to benefit-sharing (capturing the "upside").

- The treatment of externalities in large infrastructure projects. Ways of capturing positive externalities by private project promoters and ways of covering costs of negative externalities. Implications for assessing the project viability and for decision making by the guarantee instrument.

- Continuing investigation of ongoing experiences both on the supply side (institution/ schemes granting guarantees) and on the demand side (project cases in Europe and other parts of the world).

INTRODUCTION

Analysis by the European Commission of the financing needs of trans-European networks (TENs) has highlighted the absence of adequate guarantees as an important barrier to private funding.

As one response to these concerns, staff of the European Commission, together with colleagues from the European Investment Bank (EIB), began to examine in early 1992 the case for the establishment of a new Community loan guarantee facility, which would contribute to Community policies in the framework of economic and political union. This facility as envisaged would be created by the EIB, the Commission and interested financial institutions. As well as providing guarantees on loans made by the private and public sector investment institutions for investment projects in the TENs throughout the Community (and possible connections to outside countries), the new instrument would also provide guarantees (and later equity) for SME investments, notably in areas eligible for financial assistance from EC regional policy instruments.

The study, on which this publication is based, was contracted by the European Commission to provide relevant background for developing such a facility. In the meantime some of the ideas examined in the study have found an echo at a political level and the study formed part of the analytical basis for the establishment of the European Investment Fund (EIF) agreed upon at the Edinburgh "Summit" (European Council) in December 1992.

The report examines in some detail relevant experiences of other international and national institutions (both in industrialised and developing countries) and attempts to extract some lessons for the European guarantee facility. Drawing on extensive interviews, especially but not only in the City of London, it comments on the type of private funding already available on the European financial and capital markets and examines the conditions (e.g. of maturity) that are offered by these markets. It looks in particular at the market gaps and imperfections that exist, which a guarantee facility would help cover. Though the guarantee facility to be established will support both TENs and SMEs, this study concentrates on the issue of guarantee support for TENs and related large infrastructure projects. It is noteworthy that focus on TENs is in line with the provisions of the Treaty of the Union, which specifically refers to loan guarantees as an important mechanism of support in this area. The volume of investment in TENs is projected to be considerable, with increasing recourse to mixed public/private financing.

In Chapter I, the study analyses in greater detail the need for a guarantee facility, outlining some of its benefits and desirable features, in the context of a framework that implies a growing role for private funding of large infrastructure projects. Chapter II looks at the type of private funding already available on the European financial markets, and examines the gaps and imperfections in these markets. Special emphasis is placed on the type of risks that should be covered, and on modalities that could allow risk and benefit-sharing. Chapter III examines the experience of mechanisms (such as ECO) and institutions (such as MIGA) within the World Bank. The role of financial guarantees (for example of US municipal bonds, extensively used to fund infrastructure in the US) is also studied. The possible relevance of these experiences, in terms both of operational and institutional aspects, is then evaluated. This chapter also examines a few examples of large infrastructure projects which were or are being financed by the private sector both in the developed (especially Europe, US and Australia), as well as developing countries. Renewed recent interest in this, e.g. in the US, in the World Bank, is discussed. The chapter ends with conclusions and policy implications for creating a European loan guarantee facility.

Chapter I

THE NEED FOR GUARANTEES

This chapter outlines a conceptual framework for a guarantee facility in the context of private funding for large infrastructure projects. It examines the changing roles of the public and private sectors, market failures in providing long-term loan finance and the arguments for a loan guarantee facility at Community level.

1.   The changing relationship between public and private sectors

At one level private financing of major infrastructure projects is not a new phenomenon. Especially prior to World War I, railways, roads, power plants, etc., were being built all over the world financed largely by private capital, provided by entrepreneurs willing to risk all in return for high rewards. After the First World War, (especially in Western Europe) most public works were commissioned by the State and by public utility organisations; since the 1980s, however, there has been renewed interest by governments - in both developed and developing countries - in encouraging private sector investment in large infrastructure projects, both a) because the private sector is argued to bring specific management skills, to be more cost-conscious and therefore more efficient and, perhaps more importantly, b) because of a wish to alleviate government finances. However, relatively few investments of this kind are actually being carried out, though efforts are growing in this direction (see below for examples in developing countries, and in developed countries, especially the USA). There seem to be two fundamental reasons for this. One is that long years of public ownership have led to a shortage of private sector experience of investing in and managing infrastructure projects; as a result, equity finance in particular is somewhat difficult to arrange, partly because natural owners seem to be missing. Second, even after an appropriate ownership structure has been devised, private investors (nowadays, as opposed to the pre-World War I period) are unlikely to wish to carry all the risks. Thus, to ensure private investment, some form of government re-involvement is required, either as risk partners or as exclusive bearers of certain categories of risk, or during certain periods of private investing and lending. It is particularly in this latter, rather complex and fairly new aspect, that a guarantee facility can play a key role in encouraging private finance. Such limited government support seems particularly crucial when a new, fairly large involvement is desired from the private sector, as is the case of private funding for massive TEN investment required in the context of supporting the Single European Market.[1]

2.   Market failure; the case for limited public intervention

There is a strong general case in any country for some government backing to encourage private lending/investing into major infrastructure projects. This need derives from specific limitations on private financial markets in relation to five sets of factors.

First, and perhaps most important, big infrastructure projects often take a long time to build up revenues and become profitable; these time-periods are often far longer than those for which the capital or insurance markets wish to lend for or insure against. Financial markets do not wish to commit themselves over very long periods, as they seem to perceive that risk increases over time.[2] Furthermore, not only are maturities in which the investment becomes profitable long, but also most infrastructure investments have a long and sometimes problematic preparation and construction period before even starting to yield a cash flow, and therefore the eventual return may be frustrated by difficulties and risks encountered in the early life of the project. Indeed, private funding/insurance for franchises of already-built infrastructure projects is far easier to obtain than funding/insurance to include the construction phase.[3] This difficulty is further compounded by the fact that the

---

1   See, for example, CEC "Towards Trans-European Networks: for a Community Action Programme". Brussels, 10 December 1990. The concept of TENs and the difficulties they face are outlined at Annex.
2   Interview material.
3   Interview material.

finance required (loans/investment/equity) is often very large, which makes them even more difficult to raise.

Second, unlike in other sectors such as industry, agriculture or mining - where there is likely to exist an established investor who has a natural interest as well as an established track record in that line of business - there is at present in most countries an absence of such natural private ownership for infrastructure investments. This is largely because the combination of widespread public ownership and operation of infrastructure projects by the public sector has been the norm in the post-war period. As a result, there is still a relative shortage of commercial investors with genuine long-term interest in the promotion, ownership and operation of infrastructure. This makes structuring the equity component and the ownership arrangements considerably more complex. Public involvement, e.g. via a guarantee facility, may help - by providing a focal point - to put the parties together.

Third, both the length of the maturity (accompanied by high capital costs) and the very nature of infrastructure projects, imply a large number of political risks broadly defined, which have bearing on the ultimate profitability of the project. These include, for example, the regulatory framework (especially in respect of tariff and competition policy), possible dominance of the public sector either as suppliers of inputs and/or purchasers, and possible vulnerability of infrastructure projects to public criticism and government intervention, given their size, importance and visibility. Because of these types of issues, the comfort provided by public guarantees is particularly welcome to the private sector in infrastructure projects.

Fourth, in certain countries in the European Community, domestic capital and financial markets are relatively "underdeveloped", while country risk is perceived by international capital and financial markets to be higher than elsewhere, which means that relatively shorter maturities are available from private markets. There is therefore a particularly strong case in those countries for public indirect intervention (via a guarantee facility), with the purpose of encouraging private finance for large infrastructure projects, thus helping to reduce direct public intervention via direct government funding.

The argument about relatively lower levels of development of financial markets in some Community countries is expected to be a temporary one; as financial integration within the Community grows and as markets and economies of the relatively poorer countries develop.

Fifth, the case for indirect public intervention (via guarantees) is further strengthened by a failure by private financial markets to capture externalities, such as those increases to welfare provided by certain positive environmental implications of particular modes of transport or by additional external positive economic effects captured by other private economic agents and not directly reflected in income to the infrastructure project.

3. Market need; difficulties in private banking and insurance

The creation of Europe's Single Market and other developments, is significantly augmenting the demand for funds necessary to build or upgrade international and national infrastructure within the EC. Similar needs are arising in other parts of the developed and developing world. This happens at a time when, for cyclical reasons (the recession and deteriorating quality of many bank assets), as well as for more structural reasons (e.g. capital adequacy requirements, restrictions on large exposures), the banking industry's capacity (both in Europe and worldwide) to provide such funds is not only not growing as the same rhythm as demand, but may actually be contracting. The private insurance market is experiencing similar conjunctural as well as structural difficulties. The increased demand for funds for large infrastructure projects therefore coincides with a serious and increasing difficulty in supplying sufficient private finance, especially on acceptable terms.

4. Specific arguments for Community involvement

Within this broad context, there are particularly strong reasons that justify Community involvement in helping to meet the needs and to correct the failures.

The Community's means of intervention in support of infrastructure investment have hitherto been of two basic kinds: direct budgetary support (grant aids, usually in co-financing with Member States) and Communty loans (notably from the European Investment Bank, but also from the ECSC). Table 1 summarises the existing and planned provisions for these two kinds of support. Only to a limited extent has the Community's financial muscle been used to provide security for investment finance, principally through the provision of guarantees of last resort by the Community budget on lending operations of the EIB *in third countries*.

Discussions on the role of the Community in helping to fund TENs have, however, opened the way to an exploration of how to "comfort" private sector investors in major projects *within the Community* without large expenditure on grant aids and without large potential future calls on the Community budget, which is likely to be severely stretched in other ways during the coming years. Thus the Maastricht Intergovernmental Conference envisaged in the Treaty on European Union that henceforth (outside assisted areas) Community support for TENs should be concentrated on the provision of guarantees, alongside the funding of feasibility studies (to help get projects off the ground) and interest-rebates (to soften the terms of loan finance).

In theory, such guarantees could be provided by the Communty budget on a parallel with the guarantees of the EIB's external operations. But the operations envisaged are rather different. In the case of external lending support, the budget acts as a guarantor of last resort covering essentially "sovereign" risk that the Government or a National Bank in a third country may not be able to meet its debts. In the case of TENs in the Community, however, the questions posed have more to do with the sharing of perceived commercial and "policy" risk affecting companies and financial institutions, which may be better handled by a professional institution, specialising in risk assessment and management.

The case for establishment of such an institution at Communty level is partly based on the importance of properly reflecting the Communty dimension (TENs are vital to the functions of the internal market and to economic growth). It also derives from the additional risks that may be encountered by transnational projects or projects that are part of Community-wide systems. Their cross-frontier or transnational nature pose special interface risks, due to differences between countries (for example in tax, regulatory and legal aspects as well as in financial market development). Thus, already complicated financial packages at a national level become far more complex to arrange the more countries are involved. As a result, the risks and the costs of arranging such packages increase, as does the time required to do so.

The case for Community action is further strengthened by the fact that institutionalised private "markets" for guarantees either do not at present exist or do not exist to the same degree in different European countries. Furthermore, as we will discuss below, such "guarantee markets" seem far more developed in other regions of the world, and particularly in the US, than within the EC. A guarantee facility could therefore play an important role in helping to develop and deepen private markets for guarantees in Europe. If very successful and if private markets respond well, such a facility (or at least the public component in it) might only be necessary for a transitional, albeit perhaps lengthy, phase.

Table 1: EC FUNDING OF TRANSEUROPEAN NETWORK PROJECTS - MAIN INSTRUMENTS

Instrument	Type and Sector of Intervention	Geographical Coverage	Financing Limits	Overall Volume
Structural Funds	Grants only (large network projects are only one possible beneficiary of funds)	Developing, depressed and rural regions eligible for Community assistance	Max 50 - 75% of total cost depending on region	1993: 20.2 billion ECU 1994 - 1999: 141.5 billion ECU
Cohesion Fund	Grants (only for TEN transport projects and for environment)	Ireland, Greece, Portugal, Spain	80 - 85% of total public expenditure. No co-financing with Structural Funds.	1993: 1.5 billion ECU 1994 - 1999: 15.15 billion ECU
Specific TEN budget	Grants, primarily for feasibility studies, guarantees and interest rebates. All TEN sectors	All Community	Max. 25% of total cost (50% for preparatory studies)	1993: 209 MECU 1994 - 1999: Budget to be determined (around 3 billion ECU)
EEA Financial Mechanism (funded by EFTA States)	Grants and soft loans (rebate of 2%) Transport projects a possibility (along with environment, education and training)	Ireland, Northern Ireland, Greece, Portugal, developing regions of Spain	As for Structural Funds	1993 - 1997: 500 MECU grants 1.5 billion ECU loans
European Investment Bank (normal facilities)	Medium and long-term loans All TEN sectors, along with other infrastructure and productive sectors	All Community	Max. 50% of total cost. Ceiling for loan/grant combinations normally 70%	1992: 4.5 billion ECU No ex ante ceiling
European Investment Bank (Edinburgh Facility)	Medium and long-term loans Priority to TENs	All Community	Max. 75% of total cost. Ceiling for loan/grant combinations 90%	1993 - 1994: 5 billion ECU
European Coal and Steel Community	Loans under Art. 54 of Treaty related to consumption of Community steel	All Community	Max. 50% of fixed cost	1991: 505 MECU disbursed No ex ante ceiling, but volume constrained by other calls on ECSC resources and available reserve fund.

Source: EC Commission.

5. Leverage provided by guarantees

A fundamental justification for any guarantee facility is its potential for freeing public expenditure resources. The public resources required to back a fund would be small in comparison with direct public financing of the investments concerned since the exposure of any fund will be a multiple of its own resources. By stimulating private funding, it reduces the need for grant aids; it also obviates the necessity of Government guarantees themselves.

The potential leverage on private sector investment depends on the form which guarantees take and the rules of portfolio management that apply. Normally, the guarantees of any such fund would be partial; thus, the totality of investment supported would be higher, perhaps considerably higher, than the fund's exposure. Secondly, in many cases it will be possible to defer a call on guarantees (e.g. the case where the guarantee relates to the later years only of a long-term loan). Third, additional leverage can be provided by re-insurance on the private market. As regards re-insurance, the private market often insures for a limited time period (e.g. 3 years), but under certain circumstances and for certain risks, there can be surety that the private market will roll-over the insurance. When and if such is the case, the leverage would potentially be infinite!

6. Concluding comments

A clear case therefore emerges for the need of a guarantee facility to help encourage and catalyse private sector funding of large scale projects in a rapid way, at appropriate terms (especially sufficiently long maturities and possibly even somewhat lower interest rate costs).

A word of caution is, however, important. An essential part of creating such a facility is to define carefully and to specify the type of risks which such a guarantee facility would cover. Experience from other facilities shows that it is important to cover only risks, which the market would not normally cover by itself, for example due to limits of total capacity, given the size of projects and maturity involved, or given the international character of projects, as occurs in the case of the insurance market. By doing this, a guarantee facility ensures additionality. A guarantee facility, moreover, should be careful not to cover risks that should not be covered, or provide guarantees for projects that should not be done, because they are technically or commercially not viable. By avoiding taking both undesirable risks or guaranteeing an undesirable project, a Community loan guarantee facility would avoid the risk of "adverse selection" (that is taking on mainly bad risk) and of "moral hazard" (that is encouragement of non-commercial behaviour, by private actors, because they know they will be bailed out). The issue of risk is examined in more detail in the next chapter.

Chapter II

THE ISSUE OF RISK

In this chapter, we analyse how a loan guarantee facility would support the market mechanism in enhancing private financing of infrastructure investment. We start by outlining how privately funded large infrastructure projects are structured and then examine the important issue of risk associated with these projects.

1.   Project financing for infrastructure

To understand the type of private funding available, and gaps within it, for financing large international infrastructure projects in Europe, it is important first to describe the techniques used.

New techniques for providing substantial project financing for major privately owned projects, particularly in the area of oil and gas exploration and extraction, were developed already in the 1970s. In the US, and some other developed countries, similar project financing techniques have been applied to numerous privately promoted infrastructure projects, involving power plants, waste disposal facilities, bridges, tunnels, toll roads and office buildings. As these techniques evolved, the BOT model and expression was coined in the early 1980s by Turkey's Prime Minister Ozal, to designate a "build, own and transfer" or a "build, operate and transfer" project.[4]

The BOT approach is more a rediscovery than a new approach, as there is nothing particularly innovative about the provision of infrastructure services through the private sector. This is especially the case in the US[5] where there are at present some 200 private suppliers of long-distance telephone services. According to UNIDO, op.

---

4   D. Suratgar Special Risks and Security Issues in Build, Operate and Transfer Infrastructure Projects, paper presented at the Second International Construction Projects Conference, 1989, London.
5   UNIDO Industry and Development. Global Report 1991/2. UNIDO, Vienna.

cit., the average municipality in the United States contracts out 20 to 25 per cent of its services in whole or partly to the private sector (including services such as airport operations, waste collection, transport operations, road building and repair).

The current BOT model of project financing has evolved from two legal concepts, namely "concessions" and "no recourse or limited recourse" financing. "Concessions" are legal agreements where private businesses are awarded the right to build and operate railways, tramways, waterworks and other infrastructure projects. In "non-recourse or limited recourse" funding, lenders look to the anticipated cash flow of a project for repayment and servicing of the loan and to the assets of the project entity as collateral for the loan. Lenders have no (or limited) recourse to the project sponsors for the repayment or servicing of their loans. However, through security packages and risk distribution mechanisms, the recourse of lenders with regard to certain risks may subsequently be shifted to guarantors, sponsors and other parties.

Under the BOT approach, one or more sponsors from the private sector are authorised to create a private "project company" to build a project. The project company will own and operate the facility for a period of time, intended to be sufficient to pay off debt incurred and provide a reasonable return to the equity investors; at the end of this period, the project company will transfer ownership of the project to the host government.

BOT projects use a variety of sources of finance, relying both on debt and equity capital. Particularly where projects are very big, the financial packages tend to be very complex and sophisticated. The main sources can include private investors (ordinary and preferred shareholders), commercial banks, investment banks, bond markets, risk capital sources, export credit agencies, multilateral agencies, lessors, suppliers and buyers.

True private risk capital (as provided directly by entrepreneurs and as was available in the 19th century) is now extremely rare, as markets are dominated by institutions that look for a safe investment for their funds. For this reasons, perhaps the key task in a BOT project is to devise an adequate security structure, particularly for non-recourse or limited recourse lenders.

The ratio between debt and equity capital varies with projects, as do many other features of the financial engineering of projects. Indeed, it is theoretically possible to finance a project entirely from debt without there being any requirement for equity. According to Haley,[6] in the case of the Dartford Crossing, the limited recourse risks was passed on to the debt providers, who take the risk that the tolls will not be sufficient to repay the debt by the end of the concession period.

In most cases, however, there is a mix of debt and equity. The ratio of debt to equity may be lower if subordinated debt is treated as equity. For the Channel Tunnel, for example, the debt-equity ratio was 83:17 when subordinated debt is taken as debt, and 80:20 if it is taken as equity. Potential sources of equity investment include public share issues, participants in the project (such as contractors, operators and banks), institutions such as pension funds, governments and international institutions.

In a BOT project when the project proposal fails to deliver an adequate return, an element of grant (public finance) may be needed to complete the equity component of the total cost of the project (the "equity gap") in order to persuade the private sector to fund it. A key objective is to analyse critically and *minimise* this perceived "equity gap", notably through careful management of the bidding process for the project concession and precise project definition designed to put downward pressure on projected costs. The "equity gap" can be financed by a grant (for instance EC funds) and/or indirectly by a special fee levied on related or ancillary services, the proceeds of which are earmarked for the project.

---

6   G. Haley "Private finance for transportation and infrastructure projects: a view". JPMA. May 1992.

The source of revenue for a BOT project company is normally either a long-term contract with the government (contract-tied revenues) or direct sales of a service to customers (market-tied revenues). In many infrastructure cases, complex agreements between governments and the project company are required to regulate tolls and ticket revenues.

Important recent examples in Europe of BOT projects are the Channel Tunnel (by far the most important one), Dartford Crossing and the Severn River Crossing. When the Channel Tunnel is completed in 1993, it will be the first European project of an international nature, and on a massive scale, to be funded solely from private sources.

2. Types of risks to be covered

In the private funding of major capital-intensive projects, risk analysis has to be dealt with in a particularly rigorous and well disciplined manner, for several reasons[7]:

- i) combination of high capital costs and low normal operating cost implies that financing costs are a very large proportion of the total;

- ii) long construction periods, combined with the fact that the main financial commitment occurs at the beginning - this is in contrast with other investments;

- iii) both lenders and investors need to rely on the project cashflow for their return - unconditional unlimited financial guarantees are hard to obtain.

A typical infrastructure project has at least three clearly distinct phases, in which different risks need to be faced, and where different sources of funding may be involved. These are: the **promotion and preparation phase**, the **construction**

---

7   See also, R. Mathrani "Private funding of large infrastructure projects: Risk constraints and how to overcome them". Paper presented at EC Workshop on Guarantees for Funding Large Infrastructure Projects Inside the European Community. 11 and 12 June 1992. Brussels.

phase, and the **operating phase**. Because of the varying characteristics of these phases, both equity investors and lenders can be expected to seek different rewards and require different guarantees, depending upon which of these different phases they are required to participate in.

A summary of the main risks is given in Table 2 on page 22

In each stage, both commercial and political (in the broad issue) risks can be found. Political or "policy" risk, within Community countries, would tend to be related mainly to the broad institutional and regulatory framework/s within which the project would operate.

As far as the **first stage** is concerned, it may be useful to distinguish in some cases between a sub-stage where broad options are defined (e.g. bridge vs. tunnel) and a second sub-stage, where competitive bidding takes place within an already pre-defined option, and possibly with a pre-determined number of bidders. To eliminate the possibility of funding open-ended costs, public support (as discussed in the next paragraphs) may for example support competitive bidding in the second sub-stage only. Furthermore, the government may award a concession only on a route or project, which not only is well designed, but also has received environmental and planning clearances.

As regards this first crucial stage, a number of measures may be taken to fund competitive bidding (as by helping competition, either cheaper and/or better quality projects could be found). This is very important because promoters are often reluctant to embark on such projects in view of the enormous costs required to reach the start of the construction stage; costs are particularly high in cases where a specific road or rail scheme has to go through an extended process to obtain planning consent and a public enquiry.[8] Satisfying environmental concerns and legislative delays often add to the costs of this phase and substantial up-front costs

---

8   Particular problems have arisen in this respect in the UK

may be incurred, often over a fairly extended period[9]. There may be no guarantee at the end of that period, that the concession will be won or even the investment take place.[10]

Different mechanisms have been envisaged to provide partial reimbursement of investors for preparation and promotion costs. A scheme is already being applied in Greece to the Spata airport project, where a special government fund exists, to help cover a share of the cost of unsuccessful bidders. The difficulty of such mechanisms is to limit the "incentive to fail". Such arrangements should therefore provide only part of costs of bidding, up to a pre-fixed ceiling.

Alternatively, mechanisms may be found so that each bidder includes in the cost of his bid a provision to cover some share of the losses of losing bidders, which would be paid by the winning company. To make such a mechanism feasible, the number of bidders needs to be limited. Theoretically, a guarantee facility could for example provide guarantees on finance raised by the winner, if necessary, to make such payments to individual bidders.

A more conventional involvement of public institutions in cheapening the total cost of bids could come, however, through the financing or part-financing of environmental studies, traffic forecasts, etc., or other "feasibility" assessments. As noted earlier, the Maastricht Treaty already points in this direction.

In the case of international projects, there can be additional risks, because of the need to sort out these problems in more than one country. This is well illustrated by the Channel Tunnel project, where there was the risk that governments would not enact the necessary legislation to allow the required extension of boundaries. In this

---

9   For example, the period between the initial concept and the start of construction, for the privately financed Birmingham Northern Relief Road, was reportedly as long as five years.

10   Suratgar, op. cit., quotes several cases where sponsors have spent up to around $10 million just to develop a large project, in some cases, without the attempts being successful.

case, the insurance market covered against that risk[11]. Other cases could possibly arise, however, where the insurance market would be unwilling to provide this cover, and a guarantee facility could step into secure some of the finance raised to meet expenditure in the period of legislative uncertainty.

As the **second stage**, risks both of a commercial and a policy nature may be particularly high.

The principal risks are delays in commencing construction, cost overruns and delays arising from force majeure. These risks can be placed in the category of construction and completion risk, defined as the risk that the project will not be completed on time and for the price stated. This risk is normally covered by a fixed price, firm date, lump sum turnkey construction contract, often supplemented by performance bonds. As Mathrani, op. cit., rightly stresses, the experience of Channel tunnel has confirmed financiers in the need for such fixed price turnkey contracts, with stringent penalties for delays. Naturally, the price of the turnkey project is increased to compensate for the contractor taking the risk. Completion risk is secondarily assumed by the project company, and indirectly by its equity investors. Some reliance can be placed on the private insurance market, which will insure against specific risks; for example, there is a small market offering insurance cover against the financial penalties likely to be incurred stemming from some of the risks of late completion, including technical non-performance and contractor or supplier lateness. Performance bonding and professional indemnity insurance will provide further means of recourse in this area, although some risks will remain to be covered by investors and their financiers.

Most commercial banks and other lenders are themselves unwilling to assume remaining construction and completion risk. One option is to arrange commercial stand-by subordinated debt financing; however, such financing requires high interest rates and commitment fees for the risks being undertaken. Stand-by equity

---

11   Source: interview material

commitments by sponsors are also possible, but could again be very costly (with estimated annual returns in the EC for venture capitalists in a private infrastructure projects being above 30-35 per cent for such risks).

To the extent possible construction and completion risk can be taken up by the different parties involved through the mechanisms described above (with particular risks assumed by the party within whose control the risk most lies). *Blanket* guarantees against construction and completion risk should therefore be avoided by a Community loan guarantee facility, as these could become very costly and would generate "moral hazard" problems (contractors making less effort to finish on time, as they have such a broad guarantee). [12] But a loan guarantee mechanism could play a useful role in offering partial cover against specific and more narrowly defined risks, as a complement to other risk-sharing mechanisms. It could provide cover against certain risks outside the control of contractors/concessionaries, e.g.: risk of non-completion of associated infrastructures (connecting/approach roads etc.) which are built by third parties; other policy risks (changed environmental regulations etc.); and, conceivably, inflation, exchange rate or interest rate risk, alongside normal hedging arrangements. The latter macro-economic risks apply equally to the operating phase (see below). Again these problems can be exarcerbated in the case of a transnational project.

The **third operating stage** has relatively lower risk, as all the construction risks have been eliminated. As a result, certain lenders or investors, such as pension funds and insurance funds, are willing to commit resources on a long term basis, once the building stage of an infrastructure project has been completed; indeed, it is even possible that such sources would be willing to commit funds, just as the construction phase is being completed. Similarly, "monoline insurers", who provide a financial guarantee in the US or Europe that insures the timely payment of principal and

---

12 The potential costs of governments guaranteeing completion risks are illustrated by the large losses which the UK ECGD (Export Credit Guarantee Department) incurred in the seventies in its guarantee of British contractors' performance bonds.

interest in the event of bond issuer's default, tend to provide cover in many projects only once the construction is finalised.

Amongst the risks that affect a large infrastructure project in this third phase are the following:

a) factors affecting operating returns: notably technical risk that the facility does not perform at rated levels and/or has higher than planned maintenance costs; market risk (shortfalls in demand compared with market forecasts); other risks on revenue (political unwillingness to raise tolls and tariffs because of public sensitivity); the risk of operating in a regulatory environment that may be untried and/or subject to government intervention or alteration (e.g. changes in safety rules, or environmental regulations).

b) risks arising from dependence on public sector purchases of output or suppliers of inputs, such as for example, fuel for power generation.

c) risks arising from possible changes in public transport policies which could for example discourage/decrease the number of private cars driving in a toll road, thus adversely affecting expected revenues of the project.

d) externalities adversely affecting costs (e.g., measures to offset a newly perceived negative environmental effect) or having a potentially favourable effect on returns (e.g., higher land values along a new toll road corridor. The latter is for example an important element in the building of toll roads in California - see chapter III).

e) risks arising from potentially competing investments. For example, a government might license a competing facility (e.g. a parallel road) that cuts into a market, or could set user charges of a competing facility at a level so low that it will discourage use of a particular investment.

While the clearly commercial risks should in most cases, as in the previous phase, be taken by private investors and lenders, "broad political risk", related to government intervention (such as setting of road tolls, electricity tariffs, changes in taxation, changes in environmental regulations, changes in transport policy, changes in

Table 2: A TYPOLOGY OF SPECIFIC RISK

PROJECT PHASE	RISK	POSSIBLE SOURCES OF COVER
1. Promotion and Preparation	Failure of feasibility study	Loan guarantee mechanism unsuitable; public sector may co-finance in certain cases.
	Unsuccessful bid	Loan guarantee mechanism probably unsuitable; partial defraying of expenditure by successful bidder or public funds conceivable.
	Planning/environmental consents delayed or not obtained; other legislative difficulties	Possible candidate for insurance cover and for contractual agreements with national authorities. Loan guarantees might be involved as a complement depending on financing arrangements.
2. Construction	Delays and cost overruns attributable to contractors; technical non- or under-performance.	Commercial risks best covered by fixed price contracts and/or performance bonds. Insurance market for technical risks.
	Delays due to force majeure (fire, accident, etc.)	Insurance Market
	"Policy" risks (e.g. non-completion of associated infrastructure, changed environmental regulations, transport policy development)	Coverage in part by contractual arrangements with national/regional authorities and stand-by credit. Loan guarantees could play a valuable complementary role.
	Inflation/Currency Risk/Interest rates	Role for loan guarantees alongside hedging arrangements, etc.
3. Operating	Technical difficulties	Loan guarantee mechanism unsuitable. Matter for contractor/concessionary.
	Revenue shortfalls and excess costs for commercial reasons (low levels of traffic etc., changes in prices of inputs, staff costs)	Commercial risks should normally be borne by contractors/concessionaries. Some aspects may be covered by concession agreement (e.g. variable tolls). Loan guarantee mechanism might exceptionally share some risks
	Revenue shortfalls/cost overruns due to "policy" changes (competing infrastructure, environmental regulations)	Loan guarantees could play a useful role along with national/regional administrations.

government competition policy in relation to the project, etc.) might be candidates for guarantee support from a new facility.

Here too, an important area of risk, also related to government action, is that of adverse inflation, interest rate and exchange rate movements; especially in the case of transnational projects, these risks become higher and more complex to manage in all stages of these projects.

At the beginning of the 90s, there was a strong support in the financial community for the view that exchange rate risk within the European Community was very small, mainly limited to the poorer economies and would tend to diminish as the EMS was consolidated. By late 1992, the turbulence within the ERM leading to the devaluation of several currencies as within a short period, the departure of the British Pound and the Italian Lira from the ERM, and the imposition of some exchange controls in Spain, Portugal and Ireland altered perceptions. The question of providing guarantees against exchange rate volatility risk is therefore no longer academic. A loan guarantee facility could play a role in relation to changes in major economic variables of this kind. But wide coverage against exchange rate fluctuations, inflation or interest rate changes would be impracticable and extremely costly. Support from the facility should therefore be complementary to other mechanisms normally used by companies (hedging, swaps, contingency cost provisions and so on).

Only in very exceptionally justified cases, moreover, should a Community guarantee tackle purely commercial risk, such as on the level of traffic. In such cases, one could envisage at most guaranteeing 50 per cent of the difference between a minimum traffic level to make the investment profitable and the actual traffic (if that is below the minimum level) so as to make investors, lenders and other private parties share in the risks.

The problems of revenue risk can also be handled through different mechanisms. Risk can be reduced by more detailed and sophisticated forecasts (with the use of techniques such as stated preference surveys). More generally, Mathrani, op. cit., and others have suggested that governments can commission independent traffic consultants to carry out detailed traffic forecasts, which are then provided free of charge as a basis on which bidders can work.

Other measures to reduce revenue risk can include: i) allowing the concessionaire to vary tolls and extend the concession period (e.g. the UK Second Severn Crossing); ii) provide (preferably partial) revenue support guarantees if traffic forecasts are below an agreed level (this occurred in the Netherlands Tunnel); iii) the government provides subordinated debt, as in the UK Second Severn Crossing. In other cases, the revenue risk is practically eliminated by government action (see Sydney Harbour Tunnel experience below).

As said above, it would seem desirable that a Community loan guarantee facility should only in very exceptional circumstances provide guarantees related to traffic risks. Such steps would perhaps be preferably taken (and only if unavoidable) by national governments. An attractive option (applied in the Channel Tunnel) is that of user agreements, in that case with British Rail and SNCF.

While it may be appropriate in some projects for a loan guarantee mechanism to limit itself to the coverage of the *specific risks* described above, in other cases guarantees of a wider nature might be envisaged. In such cases, the mechanism could guarantee (partially) to assume the responsibilities for servicing *specific debts* in the event of a project collapse for whatever reason or the bankruptcy of a promoter. A broad guarantee of this kind could be particularly useful in persuading some commercial banks (particularly those with limited experience in long-term project financing techniques) to extend the tenor of their loans. This would be of great service in the case of projects with especially slow build-up of revenues and in which banks from different countries and of varying size and experience are involved.

It should be noted also in this context that the period for which most banks are prepared to lend varies substantially across EC member countries.[13] A guarantee facility is particularly important therefore in EC countries which are either seen as more risky by lenders, or which for some reason have less developed financial markets.[14] A Community loan guarantee facility would therefore provide an important role of helping equalise access to financial and capital markets for different Community countries.

In helping to extend the tenor of loans, a Community guarantee facility would follow in the steps of World Bank and Asian Development Bank guarantees for late maturities (see discussion below). Guaranteeing for later maturities would not only be particularly useful for certain EC countries (such as Greece and Portugal) considered "more risky" but also for Central and Eastern Europe and/or North Africa, should the projected infrastructure projects also extend to links with those countries.

It may also be important for a guarantee facility, to discriminate between sectors. For example in the UK, for certain sectors (e.g. power, "satellite telecoms"), there is at present no problem to obtain sufficient private finance quickly; however for other sectors (such as some transportation projects, water), private finance is far more difficult to arrange as returns are less clear and more long-term.

One final issue is the extent to which in the EC there is "political risk" in the narrow sense, as perceived in the context of lending to developing countries and/or Eastern Europe and CIS. Political risk narrowly defined (against which political risk insurance schemes are available in the private market) cover three types of risk: i)

---

13 According to informed market participants, in early 1992, for the UK lending for up to 18 years was feasible for good projects, whereas for Portugal it would be difficult to get loans for more than 12 years, and for Greece hard to arrange loans for more than 8 years.

14 It is noteworthy that the maximum term for Greece - 8 years - is not that much longer to that of countries outside the EEC, such as Turkey - 7 years - or even some developing countries, such as Chile - also 7 years

currency convertibility, including losses due to discriminatory exchange rates, (but excluding devaluation); ii) expropriation coverage protecting against nationalisation or confiscation by a foreign government; expropriation is defined to encompass de facto or creeping expropriation, where several governmental actions have the cumulative effect of depriving an investor of fundamental rights in an investment; and iii) political violence, including terrorism.[15] Most market participants interviewed felt that there was no "political risk" narrowly defined within the EC, but that this would obviously be an important issue if the guarantee facility was used for links with developing countries and/or Eastern Europe and/or the CIS. However, other market participants argued that such a sharp distinction could not be drawn, and that for example, the far shorter maturities at which certain EC countries could borrow reflected to an important extent, amongst other factors, perceived political risk. However, it would seem that as the process of political and economic convergence continues within the EC, then such differentials (and the perceived continuation of political risk in some countries) would tend to diminish.

As regards political risk in developing and Eastern European countries, there are several official guarantee schemes for insuring against such risk, which will be discussed below. Furthermore, there is a private market, which informed observers[16] have characterised as oligopolistic, because the number of enterprises active in political risk coverage is fairly small.[17] It is worth noting that, as different sources agree, political risk transactions on the private market must be renegotiated at least every three years. The short term cover for political risk is in part due to the renegotiating of the reinsurance treaties every year. Moreover, it matches the three

15   I.W. Cooke and T. Paefgen "Project Financing: International Legal Issues and Political Risk Insurance". Paper presented at the 1991 meeting of the International Bar Association.
16   W. Cooke and T Paefgen, op. cit.
17   Lloyds of London is by far the largest provider of political risk insurance controlling by its underwriting syndicate, specialising in political risk insurance, roughly 75 per cent of the global capacity for both confiscation and contract-frustration coverage; the total size of both the private and the government market is difficult to calculate, and crude estimates suggest annual premium income of $2b.

year accounting cycle used by Lloyds of London, in managing their syndicate books. For long-term projects that go beyond the three-year coverage period, nevertheless, a continuous cover can be obtained by means of a revolving cover facility that is carried over every year.

Besides the political risk "narrowly defined", in developing countries and in Eastern Europe and CIS, there is a set of issues, relating to whether government will fulfil its contractual obligations to a particular project; for example, in the provision of direct services or inputs, purchases of final output or promised financial partnership. World Bank guarantees against government not fulfilling such obligations play an important role in mobilising private finance for such projects in developing countries (see chapter III below).

For EC countries the risks of governments not fulfilling, for example, financial obligations to a project are far smaller, or zero. However, as pointed out above, other "broader political risk" elements are very central in Europe, and might very usefully be considered by a Community guarantee facility. These include areas such as *competition policy* (government allowing competing projects that would affect future income streams of the project and/or fixing of tariffs and tolls at levels below those agreed), and/or *changing tax legislation* in ways which significantly reduces profitability of projects, and/or *safety and environmental regulations* - e.g. speed limits on cars - that could affect levels of demand of particular projects, as well as possible changes in transport policies that could affect the number of cars driving on toll roads. As pointed out, the fact that the projects relating to TENs would involve government regulations and legislations in several countries at the same time, increases the risk and above all the complexities involved. Guarantees on those aspects would therefore perform a valuable function both in making feasible certain private funding and/or making it cheaper and/or ensuring its speedier implementation, than would be the case without it. The question is whether such policy guarantees are best assured by a financial institution charging a market rate or by political and legal commitments. A combination of the two could be envisaged.

Clearly any "political risks broadly defined" against which a Community guarantee facility would guarantee against should be as specific as possible, and be made explicit in a contractual form. Interesting lessons can be learned here from the private insurance market, about writing contracts in a clearly specified and insurable form.

3.   The sharing of risk

A basic principle in the operation of any Community guarantee facility would be a proper sharing of risk (downside) with the private sector. This might in certain circumstances be complemented by arrangements for the facility also to share in the benefits (upside), if performance is better than expected. Such arrangements would have the advantage that fees charged by the guarantee facility could be lower, and could even decline through time if the "upside" clause was triggered frequently.

It is interesting that there are European precedents in financing of infrastructure, which provide an upside element to the guarantor. Thus, in the case of the First Midland Metro, the West Midland Authority is providing some risk guarantee, and this is linked to it receiving some share of the upside.[18] In another context, the European Investment Bank, has similar schemes, with equity or quasi-equity elements included in several of its operations outside the Community.[19] Furthermore, the four California private infrastructure projects also have an upside element (see discussion below).

There are many examples in the history of large infrastructure projects, where these became far more profitable than had been expected at the time of their design and funding. A good case was the unexpected financial success of the four major bridges linking three separate islands in New York: Queens, the Bronx and Manhattan;[20]

18   Interview material.
19   Interview material.
20   Interview material. See, also, G. Marlin and J. Mysak The guide book to Municipal Bonds. The American Banker/Bond Buyer.

28

designed in the 1930s Depression, the completion of even one bridge seemed unlikely and the project was considered financially very risky. However, the projects were so successful that toll collections were soon substantially larger than annual expenditures, and the municipal bonds funding this could be repaid in eight or nine years, rather than 40 years, as had been programmed! These bridges became so profitable, that they reportedly started providing an important source of tax revenue.[21]

It should perhaps also be stressed that there are many precedents from international financial operations, which include an upside element. A recent example is in the "Brady Plan debt reduction" schemes, for middle-income countries, most of which had an upside element; thus, in the case of Mexico, the "upside" element implied an increase in the yield of the so-called Brady bonds, for up to 3 percentage points, if the price of oil exceeds US$14b a barrel in real terms (at 1990 prices); in the case of Costa Rica, the "upside" relates to a recapture clause for banks that entitles them to greater debt service payments (than otherwise would occur) under the agreement, when GDP in real terms exceeds 120 per cent of the level registered in 1989.[22]

---

21   Interview material.
22   ECLAC Latin America and the Caribbean: Options to Reduce the Debt Burden. Santiago, Chile, March 1990.

Chapter III

EXPERIENCES OF LOAN GUARANTEES

In this chapter, we review experiences relevant to the institutional set up and operational activities of a Community loan guarantee facility. We examine the World Bank Group experience, and that of US Financial Guarantees for municipal bonds; we also analyse specific case studies of privately funded infrastructure projects in both developed and developing countries and end the chapter by drawing some implications of interest for a Community loan guarantee facility.

1.   <u>World Bank Group</u>

The World Bank offers a wealth of experience on guarantee facilities of different types. We highlight here only those most relevant to a Community loan guarantee facility. Since the Bank focuses on countries (developing and former socialist), where the risks are rather different than those in the EC countries, the types of risks covered are less relevant than other aspects of the structure and functions of the mechanisms themselves.

The World Bank was originally intended to be primarily a guarantee facility to help the reconstruction of Europe after World War II.[23] In practice, however, preference was given from the very beginning to lending operations against a background of shortage of long-term investment finance and as a means of establishing the Bank's standing on the markets.

Currently, however, there is great interest both within the World Bank and by its borrowers in expanding World Bank guarantees for private sector finance. There are a number of reasons. A key one is that the World Bank can at present only lend to public enterprises and institutions. With privatisation widespread, this constrains the World Bank's potential client basis. However, a new field has opened up for the

---

23   Interview material.

World Bank to provide guarantees on loans provided by the private sector, offering protection especially against government policy changes and convertibility risks, although not against commercial risks.[24] This is particularly desirable in the growing number of cases where the government is not able to expand its own investment programme because it needs to maintain a conservative fiscal posture, and where long-term private sector funds will not come forward on a sufficient scale without some form of help. It is interesting to note that the World Bank is at present exploring with at least one government the establishment of a country guarantee facility that could be tapped by qualified projects (mainly for infrastructure) in need of long-term external debt financing.[25]

(a)   B-Loans

The new interest in guarantees has been evident for 10 years. In January 1983, the Executive Board of the World Bank approved a co-financing programme (known as the B-Loan programme), which included an element of guarantees.

A total of 24 B-Loan transactions were carried out, applying packages drawing on three techniques described in box 1, involving projects in 12 countries, and totalling $4.8 billion. Of these, 19 operations funded later maturities, while 5 funded partial guarantees of late maturities.

However, the increased incidence of interest arrears on commercial loans to LDCs in the late 1980s led to the conclusion that the sharing of payments implied in funding later maturities posed risks unacceptable to the World Bank. As regards partial guarantee support, on the other hand, prospective lenders came to view the rather narrow definition of Bank support (confined to late maturities) as too limited. An additional weakness was that the programme was geared to a narrow segment of

---

24   Interview material; internal World Bank documents
25   Interview material.

potential borrowing situations - public sector borrowings in the syndicated loan market.

B-Loans Programme   *Box 1*

Established in 1983, the B-Loan co-financing programme, allows the World Bank in addition to making its own loan for an investment project or programme (the A-Loan) to participate in a commercial bank loan for the same project or programme. The B-Loan offers three options designed to extend the co-financing instruments. These options are:

(a) direct Bank funding in the later maturities of commercially syndicated loans up to 25 per cent of the total principal amount of the loan.

(b) a Bank guarantee of up to the same amount, of the later maturities of commercially syndicated loans funded wholly by commercial banks.

(c) Bank acceptance of a contingent obligation of up to the same amount to finance the balance of principal (if any) at final maturity of a commercial loan, the annual debt service of which would be based on fixed payments of principal and interests (even though the actual interest rate would be variable).

(b)   ECO

With a view partly to broadening the scope of the World Bank's private co-financing programme and adapting it to the changing pattern of overall financing flows to developing countries, a programme of Expanded Co-financing Operations (ECO) was authorized by the Executive Directors of the World Bank in July 1989 (see box 2). The ECO allows the World Bank to extend guarantees or other forms of contingent obligations on: a) commercial loans, b) bond issues (whether publicly issued or privately placed). In the case of project finance, ECOs are seen to present a "unique way to unbundle risks by structuring the guarantee to cover only selected risks in a project. For example, the World Bank can provide targeted support in the context of limited recourse project finance for sovereign, but not commercial risks... The ECO guarantee in project financing can be similar to partial insurance rather than a comprehensive guarantee against all risks."[26]

In the almost three years of its functioning, the ECO has carried out only a limited number of operations (one of which being planned is the HUBCO project described below, another being a guarantee for a Hungarian $200m bond). An important reason is that the countries for which ECO could be used were only those: a) which had *not* rescheduled their debts in the last five years and b) did *not* have easy access to capital markets without a guarantee. The coverage of developing countries was therefore somewhat restricted, and included (in July 1991) only: Algeria, China, Colombia, Cyprus, Czechoslovakia, Fiji, Hungary, India, Indonesia, Malaysia, Pakistan, Papua New Guinea, Romania, Thailand, Tunisia, Turkey and Zimbabwe. The restrictiveness of country coverage was originally related to a wish to avoid use of ECO for debt reduction operations, in the context of the Brady plan,[27] which - it was argued - could have undermined debt and debt service reduction operations assisted by the World Bank.

Given the wish to encourage use of guarantees, the Executive Board of the World Bank approved modifications of the ECO in May 1992, which, inter alia, significantly broadened country coverage. Indeed, a number of heavily indebted or previously heavily indebted countries, such as Mexico and Chile, are now experiencing a large degree of market acceptance and voluntary finance. Some of these borrowers asked the World Bank to help them establish (or re-establish) their names in international markets and help them mobilise private capital on reasonable terms for infrastructure projects. The World Bank has therefore recently approved increased flexibility for the ECO, widening the scope of country eligibility; thus,

---

26   The World Bank Co-financing and Advisory Services Private Co-financing, September 1991.
27   Interview material.

countries which have restructured debt within the last 5 years may be considered if they have a satisfactory macro-economic framework in operation for a reasonable period of time, and have completed a debt restructuring package that has brought debt service to a sustainable level.

There is a great deal of optimism amongst Bank staff that these recent modifications will lead to a substantial expansion of ECO activities.[28]

A lesson which arises from an analysis of B-Loan and ECO facilities, in the view of informed observers and participants, is the need to keep them flexible, to leave as many decisions as possible to management and to restrict conditions established in regulations to those preserving the relevant institution's creditworthiness, and generally not to overdetermine in advance the circumstances of guarantee use.

Another lesson relates to the impact of regulatory treatment. As Bouchet[29] points out, regulatory treatment of banks' exposure is especially crucial at present, because banks need to meet the BIS capital ratios of 8 per cent of risk-weighted assets by 1993. One means of doing that is by changing the composition of their exposure. The new regulatory treatment of co-financing transactions by the World Bank does not imply risk-free assets for commercial banks' balance sheets. Indeed, bank regulators allocate a minimum 20 per cent risk weight to these transactions involving multilateral institutions; in some cases, e.g. France, co-financing operations must be weighted at up to 60 per cent. On the other hand, the guarantee by the World Bank tends to reduce spreads and fees for the bank creditors.

Other operations of the World Bank group are seen in this respect to have more advantages for the banks. Thus the extended "preferred creditor status" of IFC operations has attracted a large number of banks. The legal structure seems more

---

28   Interview material.
29   Bouchet, M. "Financial, Legal and Regulatory Issues pertaining to Guarantee Schemes: The Experience of the World Bank" paper presented to CEC Workshop on Guarantees for Funding Large Infrastructure Projects Inside the European Community. Brussels, 11-12 June 1992.

<u>*ECO - Expanded Cofinancing Operations Programme*</u>   *Box 2*

Created in 1989, the ECO programme follows the same principles and objectives of the B-Loan programme with a wider scope. It prov ides partial World Bank guarantees intended to support eligible Bank borrowers seeking to gain or improve access to syndicated commercial bank loans or international capital markets in order to attract private finance for specific infrastructure projects or investment programs that are appraised by the World Bank and are normally accompanied by World Bank loans. The World Bank guarantees cover risks not otherwise assumed by private lenders, namely government policy changes and convertibility risks. It does not cover commercial risks.

ECO guarantees on lending to public sector by commercial banks are limited to a maximum of 50% of the financing on a present value basis. However, ECO guarantees may cover up to 100% of sovereign risks on loans to private sector projects provided there is an appropriate division of risk between public and private sectors. Recently approved guidelines state that the private sector should bear all commercial risks (cost overruns), the World Bank only providing guarantees for government undertakings and not for other risks assumed by the private sector. The World Bank cover, however, should be the minimum necessary to mobilize the necessary financing for a productive purpose.

ECO on a stand-alone basis (eliminating the need for a World Bank A-Loan) may be appropriate, especially in private sector projects, provided a World Bank appraisal of the project has been carried out and other Bank procedures have been fully satisfied.

The guarantee fee is 0,5% (discounted by present value); there is a fee discount applicable for punctual borrower. There is no specific guideline as regards either amount or maturity. The guarantee implies regulatory benefits as the guarantee leads to favourable treatment under BIS guidelines (with only 20% risk factor applicable to guarantee principal).

The World Bank expects to obtain substantial leverage of its contribution to the overall package.

attractive than that of ECO. Normally, there is a single loan agreement between IFC and the borrower for the full amount of finance to be provided jointly by the IFC and by the banks. The IFC loan is divided into two parts; the first is the loan for IFC's account, and the second is funded by banks. The banks' relationship with the borrower is indirect, through IFC, which acts as sole lender of record and administrator. As a result, for regulatory purposes, no loan provisioning is required. The lesson here for a Community loan guarantee facility is that appropriate legal structures need to be defined so as to enable maximum regulatory incentives (and indirectly profitability ones) to commercial banks, to encourage their participation in desirable projects.

An important dilemma, highlighted by the B-Loans and ECO, is the tension between the need to offer a guarantee product that to be really attractive to the private sector exposes the World Bank to certain genuine uncertainties while, at the same time meeting the strict criteria of rating agencies, requiring the lowest risk portfolio and highest quality of assets, in order to maintain its AAA rating. This type of dilemma has interesting implications for a Community loan guarantee facility and its institutional set-up. It points prima facie to separation of the facility from the EIB in organisational and accounting terms.

(c) MIGA

The concept of an agency such as MIGA (Multilateral Investment Guarantee Agency) has been evolving since the 1950s although it was only established in 1988 (see box 3 outlining the main features of MIGA).

A guarantee from MIGA is particularly attractive for commercial banks in some countries (e.g. France, Spain) since these banks will *not* then need to make special provisions for developing country risks. MIGA is applying for similar treatment to be obtained in other countries, for provisioning not to be required, when MIGA guarantees are given. This special treatment is particularly valuable, to capital constrained banks attempting to meet capital adequacy ratios defined by the BIS and the EC.

Another aspect that makes MIGA particularly valuable is the fact that the potentially offending government, against whose actions guarantees are given, is a MIGA member, and therefore far less likely to take such actions.

As regards MIGA operations, these have been characterised by Mr. Leigh Hollywood, Vice-President for guarantees, as "not really a guarantee, but specific risk insurance".[30]

MIGA's standard policy covers investments for 15 years, although coverage for a project may be extended to 20 years in exceptional cases.

It has been argued that too many rules were established in the MIGA Convention concerning its operations, imposing unrealistic requirements on management, and over-determining the policies and actions of MIGA in advance. One rule that is argued by some to be too restrictive is that MIGA can be used only for new investments. A better approach, according to both outside and inside observers, would have been to only define the basic philosophic direction in the Convention, and not to have attempted to solve all future problems in advance by such detailed regulations.[31]

A rather complex set of papers has to be prepared for the Executive Board, to demonstrate that an investment is eligible. These have to show that: a) the investment is new, b) the project is developmental to the host country (looking at aspects such as employment generation, net effect on foreign exchange earnings, transfer of technology, training of employees), c) it must be financially and technically feasible, and d) it must satisfy environmental criteria.

---

30 Interview material.
31 Interview material.

Although MIGA is by its statutes a legally separate institution from the World Bank, de facto, however, it is not, as the President and the Board are practically the same. As regards the staff of the MIGA, new people were recruited rather than World Bank staff being transferred. Total staff at MIGA is only 45 employees at present; a paradoxical situation emerged when MIGA was created, as the total number of its Board members (18) was initially larger than the total of employees. So far, experience would seem to indicate the convenience of giving sufficient autonomy to staff and management in their work, and avoid excessive constraints from either the Board or even more crucially, from pre-determined rules.

Reportedly, there are complaints from potential MIGA users about both the cost and the intrusiveness of the information required.[32] There are also complaints about the length of time taken to approve a MIGA operation after the preliminary negotiations are finished (two to four months), which is apparently much longer than the time taken by private insurers to approve relatively similar operations (1 week).

MIGA's level of operations has up to now been somewhat limited, though increasing fairly rapidly. The total number of contracts executed to June 1991 were 15, for $ 191.2m in aggregate contingent liability; of these, 11 contracts were executed in Fiscal Year 1991, for a total of $ 59m; the projects insured by MIGA during FY 1991 will facilitate aggregate direct investment totalling $ 922m.

The investors that have used MIGA guarantees have come from Japan, Luxembourg, the Netherlands, Denmark, France, the US and Canada. The host countries that have benefited from MIGA guarantees are Bangladesh, Turkey, Madagascar, Chile, Hungary, Indonesia and Poland.

---

32   Interview material.

MIGA (Multilateral Investment Guarantee Agency)   Box 3

Established on April 12, 1988, as the newest member of the World Bank Group, MIGA is designed to assist developing countries to attract productive foreign investment by both private investors and commercially operated public sector companies. Its facilities include guarantees against non-commercial risks and a programme of consultative and advisory services targeted at improving the foreign investment environment in member countries.

At the time of its establishment, 29 countries ratified MIGA's Convention and their subscription amounted to 53.38% of the Agency's authorized capital of 1,082 m. In June 1991, membership had increased to 101 countries and total capital subscribed amounted to $ 789m out of which $ 155m had been paid in.

MIGA's guarantees against losses caused by non-commercial risks (political risk insurance) offer coverage against four different categories of risk which may be purchased individually or in combination, but the decision as to which coverages are needed must be made before MIGA issues its guarantees. The four categories of risks are: Currency transfer.   Expropriation. War and Civil Disturbance and Breach of contract.

MIGA can insure new investment originating in any member country and destined for any developing country.   New investment contributions associated with the expansion, modernisation or financial restructuring of existing projects are also eligible, as are acquisitions that imply privatisation of state enterprises.

Forms of foreign investment that can be covered include equity and shareholder loan guarantees issued by equity holders, providing they have a minimum average of three years. Loans to unrelated borrowers can also be covered, provided equity in the project is being also insured.   Other forms of investment also eligible are management contracts, and franchising and licensing contracts, provided their terms are for at least three years, and the investor's remuneration is tied to the project's operating results.

MIGA can enter into a variety of re-insurance arrangements, as was established by its Convention. It can thus issue re-insurance against a loss or non-commercial risks insured by national or regional entities, of member countries; it can reinsure with any appropriate entity, in whole or in part, any guarantee issued by it. It is interesting that the Convention stresses that MIGA "will in particular seek to guarantee investments for which comparable coverage on reasonable terms is not available from private insurers and reinsurers".

The total financial exposure of MIGA is determined by the limit on the level of guarantees as established in Article 22 of MIGA's Convention and paragraph 350 of the Operational Regulations. This "gearing ratio" is set as a multiple of the capital backing the Agency. Thus, unless determined otherwise by the Council by special majority, the aggregate amount of contingent liabilities which may be assumed by MIGA shall not exceed one hundred and fifty per cent of the amount of MIGA's unimpaired subscribed capital and its reserves plus such portion of its reinsurance cover as the Board will determine. The maximum amount determined by the Council shall not under any circumstances exceed five times the amount of MIGA's unimpaired subscribed capital, its reserves and such portion of its reinsurance cover as may be deemed appropriate.

MIGA has established a premium structure that provides a basis for determining the final premium rates for a specific investment; the base may be adjusted up or down for a particular project depending on its risk profile. Premium rates applicable to issued contracts are fixed for five years.

As regards links with World Bank, MIGA is a legally separate institution. Daily operations are carried out by Management supervised by MIGA's Board of 18 Directors which is basically the same Board as that of the World Bank and meets in full three times a year. Guarantees above $ 25m have to be approved by the Board.

One element that deserves some comment is MIGA's differentiated fee structure. It is interesting that in the Convention establishing MIGA, no level of fees were determined ex-ante; only the right of MIGA to establish and periodically to review the rates of premium, fees and other charges, applicable to each type of risk, was established in Article 26.

Features of MIGA's fee structure are its complexity and also its rather high level. MIGA has fairly significantly higher fees than similar national insurance agencies. One of the reasons for this is that MIGA has to break even in its operation, whereas most national guarantee agencies do not operate on such purely commercial principles.[33]

Premium rates are very tailored, distinguishing between sectors and whether the investment is at present at risk ("current") or not ("stand-by"). The "stand-by" covers for example estimated future profits and/or interest. For each risk category, MIGA can insure equity investments for up to (i) *90 per cent* of the investment contribution, plus (ii) an *additional 180 per cent* to cover earnings attributable to the investment. Similar ratios apply for loans. The investor or lender is required to remain at risk for *at least 10 per cent* of any loss, to avoid any "moral hazard". The rule that MIGA will "not cover the total loss of the guaranteed investment" is made explicit in Article 16 of the Convention. In this MIGA follows in the steps of national investment guarantee schemes which typically indemnify between seventy and ninety-five per cent of risk, to avoid "moral hazard" problems.

These operational aspects of MIGA may carry some relevant lessons for a Community loan guarantee facility (e.g. need to avoid too many rules on creation, need for agility of procedures, etc.). Furthermore, the level and variability of MIGA's gearing ratio may also be of interest to a Community loan guarantee facility; indeed, it is noteworthy that - though relatively prudent - MIGA's gearing ration (contingent liability divided by unimpaired subscribed capital and reserves) can be

---

33   Interview material.

significantly increased by the Council of MIGA, on recommendation of the Board. Though no direct lessons can be extracted on magnitudes of gearing ratio (given the different types of risk involved), the *flexibility* in MIGA's Statutes on gearing ratios may be an interesting and positive lesson.

2.   US Financial guarantees

(a)   Municipal Bonds

Municipal bonds are a very important form of funding municipal activity in the US, including investment in infrastructure projects. The total stock of municipal debt outstanding reached, in the middle of 1991, $847b, a large share of which is held by households. Most of these municipal bonds are issued by state and local governments, and are rather long-term (for up to 30 years). Such an arrangement is quite different from European traditions in municipal infrastructure financing (grants and borrowings).

Until the late 1970s, the financial guarantee market consisted of just two firms (AMBAC and MBIA) which wrote guarantees for municipal bonds. By the late eighties, there were four major municipal bond insurers in the US market. The share of these four major bond insurers, in the total bond insurance market, reached in 1987 over 95 per cent of insurance written. Only one or two more firms have joined since. The market continues to be heavily concentrated in 1990. In the early 1970s, the size of that market was $2m; by 1991, it had increased to $46b, representing around 30 per cent of the bonds issued during 1991.

The growth of the municipal bond insurance business paralleled the increase in individual investors, as opposed to institutions, in the market-place. Retail investors are particularly risk averse, and prefer to sacrifice some yield in exchange for added security.

The performance of US bond insurers is indicated by return on surplus, averaging around 10 per cent in the 1988-90 period and on return on equity, averaging around

13 per cent in the same period. As regards risk leverage (which reflects the ratio of net exposure/qualified statutory capital), this has increased over the 1988-90 period, from 117 to 132. On average, the industry paid around 33 per cent of its net income to dividends. As regards operating efficiency, a useful indicator is that which compares net operating expenses with net premiums written; this ratio averaged 38 per cent for the 1988-90 period.

The leverage of municipal bond insurers is on average around 120/130. The loss record is, till now, fairly good. The industry is assessed in-depth by rating agencies (Moody's, Standard and Poor and Fitch), and most municipal bond insurers are rated triple A. An interesting feature here is the use of "stress tests", to evaluate the effect which a major recession would have on creditworthiness of these insurance institutions.

(b) Corporate Bonds

Alongside the municipal bond market, a smaller but more diverse corporate bond insurance market has also developed.

Corporate financial guarantors conduct their business with very high leverage. It is argued that this need not imply a high level of risk, if securities insured are of "investment-grade" (low loss potential), if the portfolio of risk is not concentrated by category of risk and if credit quality is continually monitored.

Corporate bond insurers' default risk and premium levels are correlated with a variety of factors, such as governmental tax and economic policies, unemployment, interest rates, currency exchange rates, inflation and demographic trends. These risks have been moderated for those companies that have diversified their coverage by industry, geographic area, re-insurance and other factors. High quality underwriting standards are seen as the main factor limiting losses.

Most guarantees are heavily collateralised, and thus insurers have recourse to the assets underlying the debt in the event of default.

US Financial guarantees   *Box 4*

Financial guarantees are instruments of credit enhancement, which insure security purchases against default or other associated risks. They upgrade the security's rating to that of the ensurer (typically AAA), thereby lowering borrowing costs to issuers. Other associated risks insured may include currency risk, liquidity risk, interest rate risk, basis risk (the risk of loss because two interest rates may not move in parallel) and a variety of legal and fraud-related exposures. The guarantees have a wide range of maturities, going from 90 days to over 30 years.

This market was developed in the early 1970s and grew significantly during the 1980s. The industry is now large, with a total net exposure in 1990 of $372 billion, by far the largest part municipal bonds, and a qualified statutory capital of $2.8 billion.

The market consists of a rather uniform municipal bond insurance market and a corporate financial guarantee market, which is far more complex and diverse. The number of types of securities and transactions for which financial guarantees are written in the US is large; it includes long-term and short-term corporate debt, leases, receivables, limited partnership obligations, consumer receivable-backed securities, mortgage-backed securities and taxable industrial revenue bonds.

Often the main economic value of insurance to the debt issuer is that by assuming default risk, it brings improved market liquidity, lower borrowing costs, collateral monitoring services or reduces or eliminates the burdens imposed by capital adequacy requirements on issuers or purchasers of debt securities. The interest savings associated with financial guarantees can be substantial. As regards the pricing of bond insurance, premiums range from 25 points to 250 basis points, with the majority of the issues landing in the lower range.

In the US, only New York State and Florida, specifically regulate corporate bond insurance. The NY regulations require minimum investment-grade standards for all transactions, and establish capital allocation and reserve requirements, based on a number of criteria. Capital adequacy is measured relating the insurer's loss potential to total capital (surplus plus contingency reserves). New York State established standards for maximum ratio of risk to capital. Capital requirements vary between $300 of risk to $1 of capital (municipal) to $100 or risk to $1 of capital (corporate). Though useful in broad terms, these indicators are somewhat aggregate.

3. Privately funded large infrastructure projects: some case studies

In what follows we describe, in some detail, some examples of projects which have been already carried out or are being prepared which indicate different approaches to the encouragement of the private sector funding of infrastructure projects. We also refer to recent measures (e.g. legislative) taken in different countries, especially the US, to encourage private funding of large infrastructure.

(a) Developed countries

1. Australia; the Sydney Harbour Tunnel[34]

One case of private financing, which raises interesting issues, is the Sydney Harbour Tunnel, a project for which legislation was enacted in 1987.

By the early 1980s, the famous Sydney Harbour Bridge was becoming insufficient for the amount of traffic. The relevant government Department put on display several schemes, mostly for new bridges; all these attracted great opposition from local communities. The projects were estimated to cost amounts (A$500 million to

---

34 This section draws on G. Mills "Commercial Funding of Transport Infrastructure, Lessons From Some Australian Cases" Journal of Transport Economics and Policy.

A$1,000 million, at the time) that were judged to be beyond the funding capacity of the state. For both reasons, the government was unwilling to proceed.

In 1986, however, the government announced that a private consortium had undertaken a feasibility study for a road tunnel and that it would negotiate with the consortium for the construction of the tunnel, without inviting proposals or tenders from any other company. This approach goes against a basic principle of competitive bidding, which should avoid not only a priori support for a particular option (for example, a tunnel to cross a river) without looking at other options in parallel (bridges), but even more should avoid support for just one company, without asking for alternative bids.[35]

An interesting feature of the project is that the Tunnel company will receive toll revenue from both the tunnel and from the existing bridge (main features of the project in box 5). A similar arrangement has been made for the second Severn Bridge in the UK; here the company building the second bridge will also receive tolls from the first bridge.

The aim of the government was to secure the required funding for the tunnel by raising the bridge fee to an (undifferentiated) toll of $1 in 1987, and then increasing it in line with consumer prices. The government at the same time maintained discretion over the fixing of bridge tolls. The tunnel and bridge are close but not perfect substitutes. The Tunnel Act, however, stipulates that the tunnel toll cannot be higher than the bridge toll.

Although public knowledge about all the contractual arrangements is somewhat limited, (especially due to the non-competitive nature of the tendering), details are available about the financial undertakings given by the New South Wales government to the Tunnel Company. The funds available to the Tunnel Company to finance construction are outlined in box 5 on the Sydney Harbour Tunnel. An

---

35   Interview material.

important source of funds, "net Bridge revenue loan" is actually a fixed amount (independent de facto of actual Bridge revenue). Furthermore, the loan is interest free, with repayment due in 2022. Assuming a low real rate of discount and using inflation assumptions, Mills, op. cit., estimates the repayment net present value (1989) at about $40 million.

The other financial undertaking made by the government covers future revenue streams. The entire toll revenues of both bridge and tunnel are to be used to support the tunnel, during the thirty year period for which the company will operate the tunnel. The formula is complex, with both gross receipts from tolls and bridge toll collection costs based on pre-determined elements, with for example the gross toll receipts (for bridge and tunnel together) defined as the product of projected traffic volumes and a uniform (indexed, according to inflation) toll.

In certain circumstances, payments under this so-called Ensured Revenue Stream can be adjusted. These include, amongst others: a) if there is a material unforeseen increase or decrease in the cost of operating the tunnel, beyond the reasonable control of the company, payment is to be adjusted by the same amount; b) if the company fails in its claim for a deduction from its taxable income (linked to depreciation), the government will reimburse the company for the additional tax payable; c) if savings in cost of ventilation become feasible, the government may reduce payments by amounts not exceeding these savings.

These complex financial arrangements suggest that the project was not financially viable without subsidy, and possibly uneconomic. But a limited amount of grant aid allowed private funds to be raised. Without such funds, the creation of additional cross-harbour capacity would have been delayed. Another welfare point related to the economic and financial viability of the project is the fact that construction of the tunnel led to an increase in the level of the bridge toll.

As regards company incentives, cost overruns in the construction period (if due to matters under the company's control) are at the expense of the company. Thus, there is a strong incentive to manage construction efficiently. However, construction delays would not, as in a purely private company, cause a loss of gross revenue, as this would be paid by the government, independently of whether the tunnel was opened or not.

At the operating stage, the revenue will be independent of actual traffic volume. There are some modest penalties to avoid perverse incentives, e.g. the government can reduce the revenue payment if the tunnel is closed for a period over 7 days, but this is fairly modest.

As regards the government's obligations to make the revenue payments, this will be "free from any right of set-off, absolute, unconditional and irrevocable and shall not be affected by any default, event of force majeure or other event or circumstance....." This protection is very extensive, and implies the government assuming a great deal of risk. Furthermore, any adjustments in payments in favour of the government are generally to be made by the company refunding the relevant sums, with the amounts often to be determined by the company's auditors (and not by other mechanisms). This last arrangement is seen as a cause of particular worry by outside analysts.

To summarise, the risks actually incurred by the company are mainly restricted to the construction stage, and even there the risks borne (and potential penalties) are far less than in a pure private ownership. All other risks are borne by the government, and therefore by the tax-payers. There is a further complicating element in that there was no competition to select the agent; curiously, the Tunnel Company is to receive the benefits of competitive tendering for the work it proposes, but the government did not get that benefit itself! Finally, this modality may actually discourage appraisal of commercial viability, to levels below that practised normally by governments, because the outlays are off the government's budget and most of the payments are made in the future.

THE SYDNEY HARBOUR TUNNEL

Box 5

In 1986, a private consortium, the Tunnel Company, signed the concession contract with the Australian government to build and operate the Sydney Harbour Tunnel from 1992 to 2022 when ownership reverts to the government.

There are two joint ventures in the consortium: Transfield and Kumagai. Between them, they hold all the shares in Tunnel Holdings Pty. Ltd. which is the shareholder of Sydney Harbour Tunnel Company Ltd. which in turn is responsible for both construction and operation, though much of it is sub-contracted.

The Tunnel Company receives toll revenues from the tunnel until 2022 and net bridge toll revenues from 1987 to 2022. The Tunnel Act does not determine the tunnel toll price but sets a maximum, that it cannot be higher than on the bridge; the intention is to charge the same toll on the bridge and the tunnel.

The sources of funds obtained by the Tunnel Company for financing the construction during 1987-92 were the following:

- *Net Bridge Revenue "loan"*   *$ 223 million*

  (from the NSW Government)

- *Inflation-linked bonds*   *$ 394 million*

  (issued by the Tunnel Company)

- *Loan from Tunnel Holdings Pty Ltd.*   *$ 40 million*

- *Equity from the joint ventures*   *$ 7 million*

_____

Note:
The amounts shown are received at various dates during the construction period (1987-92) therefore not discounted to a common date.
Source: Mills, op. cit.

2.   Spain; the Bilbao Behobia Motorway[36]

The Bilbao Behobia motorway of some 120 kms. in length, has been fully operational since the mid-1970s. It serves an important industrial zone in Northern Spain and forms part of the international motorway linking with the French toll motorway network; for the latter reason, it is called Europistas. It is of interest because it passes through difficult mountainous terrain and provided a high-speed alternative to the existing time consuming road trunk route.

The concession concept had been introduced in Spain in 1968, as the government recognised that it lacked the necessary resources, both financial and technical, to cope with the additional demand that the motorway programme represented.

Unlike the previous case, competition was open to any competent bidder, whether financial or contractor, and competing offers were received from both financial and contracting groups.

The concession company had to enter into a full entrepreneurial role since it had not only to finance the construction, but also carry out the complete design, including the obtaining of planing approvals and then acquire land, carry out construction and operate and maintain the facility for the concession period; the concession period was for 35 years. The concession includes the commercial rights to service areas.

Financing had to be derived from both national and foreign financial markets, the latter from Euro-bonds and Euro-currency loans.

The Kingdom of Spain provided a guarantee of repayment for a part of the loan, with the commercial banks carrying the rest of the risk. No state support was given for the funding raised in the domestic market.

---

36   This section draws on J. Munro and A. McGrath "Financing Roadworks Overseas" Journal of the Institution of Highway Engineers. July 1983.

A State Exchange Rate guarantee, in return for a premium, allowed the concession to borrow in a wide variety of currencies. This was important, because at the time Spanish exchange rate risk was considered high.

Certain significant fiscal benefits are provided by the State, such as 95 per cent exemption on taxes due on interest payments, 95 per cent on import duties on plant; freedom of amortization of the investment for tax purposes was also allowed.

To reduce risk further, the Spanish State guaranteed a basic income from traffic, until a minimum viable daily flow was obtained. A formula was established to take account of effects of inflation on project profitability.

According to Munro and McGrath, op. cit., the project was built more rapidly and at less cost than would have been possible otherwise; indeed, the motorway might not have been constructed at all, without private finance.

Traffic statistics indicate rapid growth, except for a brief period of recession. The alternative trunk road was saturated by the early 1980s.

3.   United Kingdom and France; Euro-tunnel

Euro-tunnel (box 7) is the largest, single case of private investment in infrastructure in Europe. It is also perhaps the only example of privately funded transnational infrastructure in Europe involving two countries and financial institutions from many countries. The way the project is financed means that all the commercial risks are borne by private organisations. The extent to which it is, and is perceived to be, a success will have great influence on future activity of a similar kind by the private sector.

Funding

The funding arrangements for the Eurotunnel project were rather complex involving a combination of equity and loans, the latter through a syndication of 215 banks. The initial financing plan and respective sources of finance in 1987 were the following:

	£ billion	%
Equity	1.000	22%
Main loan facility	3.629	78%
(of which EIB)	(1.000)	(22%)
Total	**4.629**	**100%**

Unutilized credit availability	£ billion
Main facility	0.371
Standby facility	1.000
	1.371

There was an interdependence between the loan money and equity since loans would not have been made available unless a minimum level of equity (£ 800 m) was assured and equity would not have been forthcoming unless those who provided it were confident that enough loans were committed to complete the project.

The equity capital was planned in 3 drawdowns. Equity I amounting to £ 46 million in September 1986 was to be provided by the Founder Shareholders (the group of UK and French construction companies and banks which conceived and submitted the Eurotunnel proposal to the two governments). Equity II raised £ 206 million in capital markets in October 1986. Various difficulties emerged in this issue due to the fact that the project was still in its early stages of construction and also to some weaknesses in marketing. Equity III was issued during 1987.

The loan commitments of underwriting banks were for a total of £ 5 billion (of which £ 4.0 in the main facility (£ 3.629 b + £ 0.371 b) and the remaining £ 1 billion in a standby facility). One element that emerged during the structuring of this loan package was that the terms available from the syndicated bank market were not entirely suitable to financing projects such as Eurotunnel as there are constraints on maturities, currencies and grace periods. The structure of debt and loan amortization required was not well matched to the project's cash flow over time. It was therefore agreed that Eurotunnel would be entitled to refinance the syndicated credit through the bond market or with long-term loans after completion of construction and if the project met certain financial criteria so as to repay the syndicated loan more quickly than the final maturity provided for (year 2005) and to spread payments to refinancing creditors over a much longer period of up to the year 2035. This would also liberate more cash for the payment of dividends and increase the value of the project for investors. The EIB loan, on the other hand, had a longer maturity period than the syndicated loan and therefore was not expected to be refinanced.

Security provisions

The loan security arrangements were extremely complex involving conventional counter-guaranteeing of risk through the banking system and charges over revenues and assets (a typical project-financing approach). In the case of the EIB, the security of its loans comprises two elements: letters of credit from up to 20 first class commercial banks within the Bank Syndicate, chosen by the EIB after consultation with the Agents (to a maximum maturity of 18 years) and a pro-rata share with the syndicated banks in the charges over the project revenues and assets (valid up to year 2042).

The security arrangements made by the Banks had to take different forms depending on the location of the project assets due in part to differences between the British and French legal systems.

Concession arrangements

The concession period for Eurotunnel operating the link is for 55 years until 2042. Eurotunnel will also have the exclusive right to build and operate a road link if it accepts to do so by the year 2010. If it does not do so, then other partners will be permitted to build and operate such a road link from 2020.

The role of Governments in the concession agreements contracts with Eurotunnel was limited to regulator rather than investor or lender. In the 4 main conditions imposed by the governments, the first was that the project should be financed without any support from public funds or governments' financial guarantees and on the basis of conditions prevailing in the capital markets. The governments' undertakings in return to Eurotunnel included the following:

(a) once the concession contract had entered into force, the governments would not terminate the promoter's right to build and operate the link during the concession period unless for reasons of defense or national security;

(b) no government intervention in the conduct or operation of the Tunnel, only Eurotunnel will be free to set and follow its own commercial policy, including tariffs and the type and level of service offered (subject to competition legislation);

(c) that no other fixed link will be authorized to operate before 2020;

(d) that no subsidy would be granted for any other fixed link for 55 years (2042);

(e) equalization of fiscal treatment on the sale of duty free goods on competing modes of cross-Channel transport.

These undertakings were necessary to ensure the project to be financed as a sole private sector project.

Cost Control

A major problem with the project has been cost control. As Eurotunnel argued in its 1991 Report, "the final completion of the Channel Tunnel has been spectacularly successful in engineering terms, but at a cost of 50% over the target set".

By mid 1990, difficulties in the Eurotunnel project had resulted in total cost increase of the project to £ 8.1 billion. This was mainly due to construction costs increase of £ 1.7 billion and the remaining due to interest rates and inflation occurred during that time period. One main factor appears to have been the difficulty in mastering a project of such enormous scale and in evaluating adequately the costs from the outset which were complicated by different trends in both countries in interest and inflation rates during the construction period).

With hindsight it would seem that more time should have been devoted to the conceptual and design work. Whatever the weight of the different factors involved, new funding became necessary, involving further lending by EIB.

THE CHANNEL TUNNEL   Box 7

- *France and UK signed a treaty on 14 February 1986 to build a tunnel between the two countries: The Channel Fixed Link.*

- *The project agreement between the two countries and the concessionnaires was signed on 16 March 1986; the concessionnaires are the Eurotunnel Group, a consortium of Eurotunnel PLC, Eurotunnel SA and their subidiaries. This project agreement entitled them to design develop, finance, construct and operate the Channel Fixed Line for 55 years until 2042.*

- *Subsequently, on 29 July 1987, the Railway Usage Contract was signed between the Eurotunnel Group and the National Railways covering the terms agreed for the operation trains through the tunnel up to half the Tunnel capacity.*

- *The construction contract signed between the Eurotunnel Group and Transmanche Link covers the design and construction covering all the work. It contains three separately priced set of works, namely:*

  (a)   a lump sum for the English and French terminals and the fixed equipment in the tunnels (only accounting for 40% of the total cost of the project)

  (b)   a target price covers the tunnelling work itself

  (c)   and a provisional sum in respect of the locomotives and rolling stock.

- *The credit agreement of 4 November 1987 between the project company and a syndicate of 215 banks stipulates the conditions and type of loans and other financial instruments used in the funding of the project. The credit agreement allows for a syndicated loan with a 18 years maturity, linked with Railway Usage and with the Construction contracts, and an EIB loan of up to 25 years.*

- *Funding was provided by the original group of 5 banks and 10 contractors by way of cash contributions and by seconding manpower to the project. The original banks formed the nucleus of the banking sydicate which expanded to an underwriting group of some 50 banks which negotiated the credit agreement before the Syndication.*

The new financing plan in May 1990 was the following:

	£ billion	%
Equity	1.614	19%
Debt	7.000	81%
(of which EIB)	(1.300)	(15%)
Total	**8.614**	**100%**

Though the share of EIB loan is now smaller in the total, the participation of the Bank in an arrangement which needs particularly long-term finance to complement the syndicate, is essential if the syndicated banks are to carry out their part in financing the overall solution. The additionally planned equity will not be issued unless the syndicated banks provide the debt required and to complement the syndicate, the EIB, some major banks and long-term credit institutions can provide the long-term finance that makes viable the whole financing package.

4. United States; California Department of Transportation Toll Road Privatisation Programme

In the US there has been growing interest in getting private capital further involved in infrastructure building. This is because highway building has been at a relative standstill since the mid '70s, partly because of tight state and local government budgets, partly due to difficulties in getting environmental approvals. In California, a region growing very fast in the 1980s, the economic impact of slow-moving traffic, is immense; in Los Angeles county, many estimates put the cost of congestion at more than $ 1 billion a year in wasted time and fuel.[37]

---

37 Interview material; Forbes, April 2, 1990.

To encourage participation of the private sector in the State of California, legislation was enacted in July 1989 (AB680) enabling Caltrans (California Department of Transportation) to develop on a pilot basis, partnerships with private entities to design, build and operate four demonstration infrastructure projects to improve transportation service in California and to offer a viable business opportunity (demonstrating financial capability for development, right of way and construction costs and also for operation costs, maintenance and police services). In September 1990, Caltrans approved four private toll road projects from eight competing proposals (see box 8). According to the Assistant Director of Caltrans, the projects chosen were "the likeliest to produce almost instant high volumes of traffic or where the financial support from the landowners and the communities is sufficient to make deals financeable".[38]

The impact of privatization in the new legislation was estimated to add more than $ 160 million a year to capital spending on new transportation facilities.[39]

The main features of the operations are the following:[40] Investors would be granted leases of up to 35 years to operate the transportation facilities and to recoup their investment and project through tolls and land development revenues. As as partner in the project, Caltrans would support proposals by accelerating schedules, by negotiating equitable leases and rates of return and by reducing liability after projects are constructed. The transportation facilities developed privately will be owned by the state to which they will be conveyed as soon as construction is completed and before operation begins. The state will then lease the transportation facilities to the private builder-operator for the terms of the franchise. Lease terms and profit levels were related directly to the extent of risk taken and negotiated with Caltrans depending upon the nature of specific proposals.

---

38   Public Works Financing. October 1990.
39   Based on Privatization. January 1990. California Department of Transportation.
40   Public Works Financing op. cit.

Toll rates and fees were limited only by market conditions. Any toll revenue received in excess of financing, profit and operating cost must be applied to the indebtedness incurred by the project sponsor in developing the transportation facility or must be paid into the State Highway Account.

Projects were to supplement the existing "free" system and offer a reasonable choice (free or toll) to potential users and the public.

Project were expected to be financed by private funds. Local entities were not precluded from participating in project funding or from supporting a project by giving it high priority for regulatory approvals and permit processing. However, proposals had to satisfy state and local laws including environmental and land use regulations. Caltrans has pledged regulatory and political support.

To enhance proposals for demonstration projects, land associated with a transportation project may be developed for commercial use. Some projects may derive revenue from both the transportation facility and associated development. Non transportation facilities associated with the development of a transportation project may be leased by Caltrans beyond the 35 years lease period for the transportation facility and may be negotiated for periods of up to 99 years.

Land that is capable of development and that is located near or next to a proposed transportation facility may enhance the financial viability of a proposed privatisation project. Thus construction of the transportation facility may be considered an action that adds value to the nearby land.

Other revenues may be derived from transmission of data, water, electricity or other materials and form any other activity that is legal and profitable.

Caltrans is authorized by the enabling legislation to use its condemnation powers on behalf of demonstration projects. However, its policy is to use such powers only after a private consortium or company has made documented, good faith effort to acquire property in the open market. And if does offer this power, Caltrans' first step

The approved four private toll road projects under the legislation enacted in July 1989 by the State of California enabling California Department of Transportation to partnership with private entities in build transfer and operate demonstration infrastructure projects which will improve transportation facilities in California.

1. **Santa Ana Viaduct Express.** *A four-lane limited access, cars only express toll way in Orange County extending by 11,2 miles two existing routes. To be completed by April 1997.*

   Project Sponsor: The Perot Group consortium.   Cost estimate: $ 700 million.

2. **San Diego Expressway.** *A 10 miles limited access four-lane toll road in Dan Diego County. Expansion to 10 lanes possible. To be completed by December 1995.*

   Project Sponsor: California Transportation Ventures (Fluor Daniel Inc., Parsons Brinckerhoff Development Co, Transroute and Prudential Bache Capital Funding).   Cost Estimate: $ 400 million.

3. **Orange Lanes.** *A 10 miles extension of the high-occupancy-vehicle (HOV) lanes in the median of the Riverside Freeway in Orange County. To be completed by 1993-1994.*

   Project sponsor: California Private Transportation Corporation.
   Cost estimate: $ 88,3 million.

4. **Mid-State Tollway Project.** *A 85 mile highway built in three phases from the south esnd of San Francisco Bay north to Interstate 80 near Vacaville. To be completed by January 1997.*

   Project sponsors: California Toll Road Development Group.
   Cost estimate: $ 1,2 billion.

would be to bring the respective parties together to attempt a satisfactory resolution not requiring condemnation action.

It is worth stressing that financing will be mostly taxable securities backed solely by toll and other revenues collected by the private lessor-operators. No state or federal funds or credit can be used to support the project financing. However, municipal and country governments have pledged extensive assistance to private firms, for example, in obtaining right of way, regulatory and political support. It is this support, plus the potential for toll revenues and additional sources of income, which makes these projects particularly attractive to the private sector.

(b) **Developing countries**

1. Pakistan; Hub River Power Project

Though private financing to large projects in developing countries pose different (additional) categories of risk to lenders than those in the EC, we outline here a major private project in a developing country for two reasons. First, some of the activities of a Community facility might be geared, at least partly, to network links with East European countries, and there this example is of more obvious relevance. Second, and more broadly, the issues of how specific risk is allocated between the public guarantor/s (World Bank and possibly also Japanese Exim) and other actors (especially private lenders) is brought out in a rather interesting way by the Hub Power Company Project. The (complex) nature of both financing and risk-sharing arrangements in the project is also of general interest in our context. Details of the project structure are summarised in box 9.

The Hub River Project is far from an isolated example of interest by developing countries in promoting privately financed projects.[41] Perhaps the country with most

---

41 For an overview, see V. Richardson "Experiences of Various Guarantee Schemes" paper prepared for CEC Workshop on Guarantees for funding large infrastructure projects inside the Community. Brussels, 11-12 June 1992.

experience is Malaysia, with eight projects under construction or completed, and two completed by 1991. An interesting case is also that of the Mass-Transit System in Thailand, especially because it incorporates a large payment by the concessionaire to the government, in exchange for rights to develop commercial and residential complexes at stations through which the system runs. This reduces the total cost of the investment project, by capturing via the market locational externalities and incorporating these into the financial arrangements. As Richardson, op. cit., concludes, the decision by the Thai government to allow the contractor to capture these externalities acted as an interesting market-related financial guarantee to the project sponsors contractors.

Amongst other countries where BOT projects have been finished or are under construction, or serious consideration are: China, Hong Kong, Mexico, Chile, Singapore and Turkey.

As far as the Hub River Project is concerned, the details are not fully agreed at the time of writing, and that the project is described mainly with a view to extract relevant lessons[42] (see box 9).

The Turnkey Contract has been awarded through a competitive process.

As regards risk, there are no unforeseen risks in design and construction, as the units are based on proven technology. Risks of damage due to fire, explosion, etc., would be covered by commercial insurance provisions.

The World Bank (through its Expanded Co-financing Operation) is proposing to partially guarantee a syndicated commercial bank loan to HUBCO; another part of the guarantee would be provided by the Export-Import Bank of Japan (JEXIM). The loan will be for a term of 12 to 14 years from the date of the agreement, including several years of grace. The balance of the costs will be financed by export

---

42 Information based on interview material.

credit agencies, subordinated debt (partly funded by the World Bank) and foreign and local equity.

The World Bank and the JEXIM Guarantees will cover the principal payments due under the loan and those remaining unpaid. The Escrow Agent of the Lenders' Debt Service Escrow Account will have the authority to call the guarantee on the occurrence of certain specified events, which imply HUBCO not making principal payments (or part of them), either on scheduled payment or on acceleration, and the failure of HUBCO to pay due to failure of the Government of Pakistan (GOP) to make available equivalent foreign exchange for local currency and/or result from the failure of GOP to provide local and foreign currency payable to HUBCO within the Implementation Agreement.

The World Bank ECO would provide a guarantee in respect of 100 per cent of principal in the event of debt service default on the loan, if the default is due to the failure of the government to fulfil its obligations in the security package (outlined below). The guarantee would be accelerable at any time after the grace period. Thus, the ECO covers principal of debt service defaults arising from the failure of the GOP to carry out specific undertakings which it would underwrite; these consist of: i) Special Temporary Funding; ii) Deficit Funding in the event of occurrence of certain defined events; and iii) a guarantee for foreign exchange convertibility by the State Bank of Pakistan.

The guarantee fee (as standard in ECO operations) is 50 basis points per annum.

Pakistan and HUBCO undertake to reimburse and indemnify the World Bank for any payments made by the World Bank under its guarantee.

The security package provides the framework within which the guarantee is being proposed. Unlike other guarantee operations of the World Bank, the proposed guarantee is intimately linked to the performance of the Government of Pakistan and other public entities (such as WAPDA, PSO, etc.) under various agreements, which form part of the security package.

The project uses the build-own-operate (BOO) technique; its financing is proposed to be undertaken substantially by limited-recourse financing, under which the commercial bank lenders (and other lenders and investors) would assume full completion and operational risk, and look primarily to the expected cash flow revenues of the Project, as the basis for the borrower to service its debt. There would be no direct sovereign guarantee from the GOP. The main feature of the project is that WAPDA, a public sector entity, is the sole purchaser of the Project's offtake; its capacity to generate power is also dependent on at least two other important factors These are the fulfilment by GOP of its commitment to provide contingency funding to HUBCO (such as Special Temporary Funding, in respect of situations of Pakistan political force majeure and in the event of shortfalls in capacity/delivery of power to WAPDA or during the period of disputes, via Deficit Funding contingency). Contingency funds are also available for the case of non-performance by other public sector entities (WAPDA, PSO, etc.) and the non-fulfilment by the State Bank of Pakistan of its obligation to make available the required foreign exchange to service debt. The GOP also guarantees the performance of certain critical public sector entities (e.g. to supply fuel and purchase as well as pay for the power off-take). There is also a power purchase agreement specifying for example the level and structure of the tariff.

Private bank lending forms a key part of the financing package, though Pakistan has not in recent years been able to obtain commercial bank financing on a limited recourse basis. Indeed, even direct sovereign borrowing has been limited, both in amounts and maturities beyond one year, with only two fairly small and special exceptions.

In this context, it is interesting to stress that in the package a considerable amount of the project risk is borne by the private sector and thus is not covered by the World Bank guarantee or counter-guaranteed by the Government of Pakistan. These risks are completion and commercial risks provided the security arrangements are satisfactory. However, the commercial banks are unwilling to assume sovereign risks on long-term loans. The Government of Pakistan has agreed to guarantee the

Hub River Power Project   *Box 9*

The project consists of four oil fired electricity power generation units in a total of 1.300 Megawatt, to be sited near the mouth of the Hub River, about 40km from Karachi. This project will add 18% to the existing electricity capacity.

Fuel for the plant to be supplied by a pipeline, which Pakistan State Oil Company (PSO) will build and operate. Output of the plant to be purchased by Pakistan Water and Power Development Authority (WAPDA) which will construct the transmission facilities.

Total project cost estimated at US $ 1.54 billion in December 1991 (21% equity, 26.4% from the PSEDF and the balance from commercial loans).

To build and operate the project, the Hub Power Company (HUBCO) has been set up with participation of companies from six countries (Saudi Arabia, United States, United Kingdom, Japan, Canada and Pakistan) led by Xenel Industries of Saudi Arabia and Hawker Siddeley Power Engineering of Great Britain. The Group and the Government of Pakistan agreed in 1988 in general terms on the tariff level, plant configuration, indices for tariff inflation adjustment, indices for domestic currency adjustment to foreign currency and completion date.

Pakistan Government BOT provisions for energy generation projects.

Each private sector energy generation project to be financed with 25% equity participation in total project cost; and to involve the private sector in power project financing, the Private Energy Development Fund (PSEDF) was set up which will be managed by the Pakistan National Development Finance Corporation. The World Bank assisted in the creation of PSEDF with US $ 150 million to its initial funding of US $ 520 million. Co-financers of the Fund are JEXIM (Japan Export/Import Agency), United Kingdom Overseas Development Aid, US Aid and the Italian Government (the initial funding is sovereign guaranteed). The objective of PSEDF is to provide long-term (up to 23 years including 8 years grace period) subordinate debt financing covering up to 30% of total cost of energy BOT projects.

performance of its agencies and to provide special funding to lenders and investors against events of Pakistan political force majeure. Nevertheless, given the scale of resources required and the novelty of the deal for Pakistan (especially in the area of infrastructure), commercial banks are seen to require the comfort of a recourse if the Government of Pakistan does not comply fully with its guarantee. Thus, the GOP failure to fulfil its obligations of the security package are assumed by the ECO guarantee.

It is also interesting to note that the World Bank ECO guarantee in this case is more similar to a partial casuality insurance rather than its normal feature of a comprehensive guarantee against all risks (with a cover of 50%) since here the ECO covers only selective risks but with a 100% coverage. Though the specific risks to be covered in the EC are different to those in developing countries, this selective approach to risk is both important and relevant.

A final interesting point is that because the World Bank guarantee is a partial one, the indemnity from the Government of Pakistan to the World Bank is only limited to those risks covered by the World Bank under the ECO guarantee. Therefore, the GOP's guaranteeing limits are used to a lesser extent; also it strengthens the GOP's case for not providing full guarantees to other lenders/guarantors, either for this or other private sector projects in Pakistan.

4. Conclusions

(a) Implications from existing guarantee mechanisms

Of the experiences reviewed, there are some important features of interest for a Community guarantee facility.

As regards the World Bank, there is a renewed interest in expanding its guarantee activities. The existing schemes reviewed here were the B-Loan and ECO guarantee, the IFC co-financing as well as MIGA which is a member of the World Bank Group guaranteeing against political risk. Their experiences were somehow limited due to the relatively short period during which these schemes have been operating. Another possible explanation for the limited number of operations relates to the excessive constraints put on the operations of facilities like ECO and institutions like MIGA by too much predetermination of their activities by regulation defined and approved even before the guarantee facility/institution began to function. The lessons would be to keep a guarantee facility more flexible, leaving most decisions to the management and restricting conditions to regulations preserving the relevant credit worthiness of the institution.

The IFC extended "preferred creditor status" operation has, however, attracted a large number of bankers because its legal structure does not require making provision for loans jointly financed with IFC since the IFC acts as the sole lender of record and administrator.

The World Bank experience also showed that there exists a dilemma between the need to offer an attractive guarantee product to the private sector which exposes the World Bank to certain uncertainties and at the same time meeting the triple A rating which means the lowest risk portfolio and highest quality of assets. This makes more attractive the creation of a separate and somewhat autonomous institution which is not bound by rating considerations.

MIGA's institutional arrangements, financial and fee structure, offers interesting precedents. One such element is, for example, the gearing ratio, which was established at 150 per cent (contingent liabilities/unimpaired subscribed capital plus reserves), but can be increased up to a limit of 500 per cent, if MIGA's Board approves it. The relevance of the specific figures is somewhat limited by the specific nature of the risks incurred in MIGA, but it has interest in that it suggests the possibility of flexibility, that is of starting with a fairly conservative ratio, but allowing flexibility for increasing it, if experience indicates this is desirable.

A MIGA guarantee on loans from banks in some countries (e.g. France, Spain) means that those banks do not have to make special provisions against the loans, and that favourable treatment is given with respect to BIS capital adequacy ratios. Co-financing with the IFC has an even more favourable effect. Again this is of great interest to a Community guarantee facility, which would aim to obtain similar or parallel regulatory advantages, as these have important positive incentive effects for encouraging private finance.

The US Financial guarantee for municipal bonds has proved a mechanism with significant impact in expanding the individual investors market. In the US during the time period 1987 to 1991, households increased their share in total municipal debt from 35 to 40%. Retail investors, being particularly risk averse, prefer added security in exchange for a lower yield. It is noteworthy that this market is just starting to develop in Europe mainly via branches of US companies.

The guaranteeing of US municipal bonds is noteworthy for several reasons in this context. First, a large proportion of these bonds fund infrastructure projects, based on an interesting and rather successful tradition of such funding in the US (European parallels of raising private finance for local government infrastructure construction seem far more limited). The interest savings, which the guaranteeing of such bonds allow, are very substantial, and thus allow important cost savings to the municipalities.

The financial guarantee market offers interesting lessons and suggestions to a Community guarantee facility, 1) in terms of its operational experience, fees, gearing, criteria (limited so far mainly to the US), 2) in terms of the need to contribute to the development of similar markets in Europe where those do not exist, and 3) in terms of possible collaboration between a Community loan guarantee facility and this financial guarantee market, should such opportunities arise.

(b) Implications from case studies

There is a great variety of experience both in developed and developing countries with private funding of infrastructure.

At one extreme of the range are cases like that of the Sydney Harbour Tunnel and to a lesser extent the Bilbao Behobia motorway, which seem to imply a fairly large amount of government direct support (e.g. subsidies) and especially guarantees; the Sydney Harbour Tunnel especially includes not just guarantees against political risk broadly defined (level of tolls, etc.), but also on commercial risk, as the net revenue is a pre-determined fixed amount, independent of actual revenue, determined by actual traffic. Guarantees in the Bilbao motorway are more restricted, and seem perhaps better tailored to the specific needs of private lenders under the circumstances of Spain in the late 1960s; indeed, at that time, a government guarantee against foreign exchange risk was particularly important for Spain.

At the other extreme of the range are cases like that of the Channel Tunnel and the four California projects, where there are no explicit government guarantees. Governments were active in other ways to support private financing. In the case of the Channel Tunnel this occurred through, for example, French government investment in railway connections, in the EIB loans that are seen to have played a key role and indeed in indirect pressure to persuade private lenders. As regards the Channel Tunnel, the novelty of such an interesting project may have encouraged banks to participate; however, the perceived numerous problems, especially in the UK, may perhaps make it more difficult to fund similar projects of that scale without government guarantees. One interesting element in the funding was the difficulty for the banks to arrange long-term lending without special provisions on refinancing the complex risk-spreading arrangements among financiers.

In the case of the California projects, future profitability seems to be enhanced by the authorisation that land associated with the projects may be used for commercial development for periods of up to 99 years! Also, projects in California, given the dynamism of the region, are seen to be highly profitable by the private sector. An interesting element in the California projects is that beyond a certain level of profit there is an element of "upside", which is paid into the State Highway Account.

A very interesting, somewhat intermediate, project is that of the Hub River Company in Pakistan. Here public guarantees are involved, provided by the World Bank and JEXIM, but they neither cover broad sovereign nor broad commercial risk, but are fairly specifically targeted on aspects, such as supply of fuel by the state oil company and off-take of energy by the state electricity company. They also cover against broader risk, relevant only to developing or East European countries, related to foreign exchange availability. The more precise and specific definition of risk against which guarantees are being provided seems to offer interesting and relevant precedents to a Community loan guarantee facility. As pointed out above, because within the EC there tend not to be any overwhelming political or transfer risk as in developing countries, targeting guarantees on clearly specified risks may become both easier and more fruitful.

ANNEX

TRANS-EUROPEAN NETWORKS: THE CONCEPT AND THE CONSTRAINTS

What follows is based on the Commission document COM (90) 585 final of 10 December 1990 titled "Towards Trans-European Networks for a Community Action Programme".

The provisions of the Single Act and the guidelines set out in the Commission's White Paper of June 1985 were the basis for the single market programme.

The Commission document argues that the economic effects of successfully implementing the four fundamental freedoms of the White Paper largely depend on the existence of infrastructure networks which facilitate communication and shrink the Community in terms of time and distance, contributing also to greater cohesion.

The single market programme will therefore only generate all the economic and social effects it aims at if the free movement of

Goods
Services   *[the four freedoms]*
Capital
Persons

in an area without frontiers is backed up by TENs notably in the areas of:

Transport
Energy
Telecommunications[43]

---

43   The Commission document also refers to training networks. This is, however, not relevant to our disucssion of infrastructure questions and is therefore omitted from our discussion.

The need for such infrastructures is strengthened by the following 5 aspects based on the effects expected from the achievement of the Single Market and on the requirements for its successful implementation:

- *the predicted increase in intra-Community free trade (the volume effect)*

- *the need to draw closer together all areas of the Community space (cohesion effect)*

- *the need for existing infrastructures and services to be connected and to be able to work together to match the new dimensions of the market (interconnection and interoperability requirements)*

- *the importance of taking the Community dimension into account in the design and development of future network systems (dimension effect)*

- *the increased need for adequate service quality throughout Europe (quality requirement).*

The emergence of TENs is seen by the Commission to depend as much on private sector initiatives as on action by the public authorities, and the concept of "service (user) charges" according to which the user is prepared to pay for the quality service he receives should strengthen the private sector involvement and facilitate the private financing of the networks.

The main barriers to the emergence of TENs are the following:

Problems of interoperatibility
Inadequate legislative environment
Competition
Lack of global vision
Lack of finance

The concept of interoperability of networks in the Community means that infrastructures and their management should be able to operate inside the Community as if they were operating within national frontiers (compatible technical standards, no administrative barriers).

Difficulties of transfrontier interoperability are substantial in the areas of transportation and telecommunications. The lack of interoperability between national networks makes it impossible for them to link up with each other beyond national frontiers and to be operated simultaneously or consecutively so that they offer a coherent and satisfactory service at a reasonable cost to the user. These difficulties are linked not only to the facilities, installations and technical standards concerned but also to the services provided, as well as different national regulations and administrative provisions.

The legal environment barrier refers to the difficulties arising from the multiplicity and diversity of national administrative procedures, legal and tax systems, etc.

The competition barrier reflects the difficulty of reconciling the principle of free competition (making sure that the benefits of liberalization are not offset by monopolies or agreements) with greater integration of the networks which requires increased cooperation between the parties involved.

The principal financing barrier in relation to private finance is identified as that of high risk (long term commitment, difficulty in evaluating potential returns, the cost and the duration of construction, macroeconomic parameters, complexity of the legal and administrative environment, political uncertainties, etc.). Also the ongoing decompartmentalization of financial markets is not yet able to cope easily with trans-European project funding. The absence of feasibility studies owing to lack of funds tends in addition to delay the emergence of projects.

It is recognised that private finance is not suitable on its own in all cases and therefore public finance is needed in mixed participations (where projects do not offer sufficient rate of financial return and where it is difficult or impossible to make the user pay for the infrastructure service).

The concepts developed in the 1990 paper by the Commission were subsequently refined and developed in discussion with Member States and economic operators. The result is reflected:

Title XII of the Treaty on European Union (the "Maastricht Treaty"), which reads as follows:

"Article 129b

1. To help achieve the objectives referred to in Articles 7a and 130a and to enable citizens of the Union, economic operators and regional and local communities to derive full benefit from the setting up of an area without internal frontiers, the Community shall contribute to the establishment and development of trans-European networks in the areas of transport, telecommunications and energy infrastructures.

2. Within the framework of a system of open and competitive markets, action by the Community shall aim at promoting the interconnection and interoperability of national networks as well as access to such networks. It shall take account in particular of the need to link island, landlocked and peripheral regions with the central regions of the Community.

Article 129c

1. In order to achieve the objectives referred to in Article 129b, the Community:

- shall establish a series of guidelines covering the objectives, priorities and broad lines of measures envisaged in the sphere of trans-European networks; these guidelines shall identify projects of common interest;

- shall implement any measures that may prove necessary to ensure the interoperability of the networks, in particular in the field of technical standardization;

- may support the financial efforts made by the Member States for projects of common interest financed by Member States, which are identified in the framework of the guidelines referred to in the first indent, particularly through feasibility studies, loan guarantee or interest-rate subsidies; the Community may also contribute, through the Cohesion Fund to be set up no later than 31 December 1993 pursuant to Article 130d, to the financing of specific projects in Member States in the area of transport infrastructure.

The Community's activities shall take into account the potential economic viability of the projects.

2. Member States shall, in liaison with the Commission, coordinate among themselves the policies pursued at national level which may have a signifcant impact on the achievement of the objectives referred to in Article 129b. The Commission may, in close cooperation with the Member States, take any useful initiative to promote such coordination.

3. The Community may decide to cooperate with third countries to promote projects of mutual interest and to ensure the interoperability of networks."

LIST OF REFERENCES

Bouchet M., "Financial, Legal and Regulatory Issues pertaining to Guarantee Schemes: The Experience of the World Bank" paper presented to CEC Workshop on Guarantees for Funding Large Infrastructure Projects Inside the European Community. Brussels, 11-12 June 1992.

CEC, "Towards Trans-European Networks for a Community Action Programme". Brussels, 10 December 1990.

Cooke I.W. and Paefgen T., "Project Financing: International Legal Issues and Political Risk Insurance". Paper presented at the 1991 meeting of the International Bar Association.

ECLAC, Latin America and the Caribbean: Options to Reduce the Debt Burden. Santiago, Chile, March 1990.

Euro-tunnel, Interim Report. 1991.

Financial Times, 20 February, 1990.

Forbes, April 2, 1990.

Haley G., "Private finance for transportation and infrastructure projects: a view". JPMA. May 1992.

Marlin G. and Mysak J., The guide book to Municipal Bonds. The American Banker/Bond Buyer.

Mathrani R., "Private funding of large infrastructure projects: Risk constraints and how to overcome them". Paper presented at EC Workshop on Guarantees for Funding Large Infrastructure Projects Inside the European Community. 11 and 12 June 1992. Brussels.

Mills G., "Commercial Funding of Transport Infrastructure, Lessons From Some Australian Cases" Journal of Transport Economics and Policy. 1991.

Munro J. and McGrath A., "Financing Roadworks Overseas" Journal of the Institution of Highway Engineers. July 1983.

Privatization, January 1990. California Department of Transportation.

Public Works Financing, October 1990.

Richardson V., "Experiences of Various Guarantee Schemes" paper prepared for CEC Workshop on <u>Guarantees for funding large infrastructure projects inside the Community</u>. Brussels, 11-12 June 1992.

Suratgar D., <u>Special Risks and Security Issues in Build, Operate and Transfer Infrastructure Projects</u>, paper presented at the Second International Construction Projects Conference, 1989, London.

UNIDO, <u>Industry and Development. Global Report 1991/2</u>. UNIDO, Vienna.

World Bank, Co-financing and Advisory Services <u>Private Co-financing,</u> September 1991.

European Communities — Commission

Loan guarantees for large infrastructure projects: the issues and possible lessons for a European facility

Luxembourg: Office for Official Publications of the European Communities

1993 — 100 pp. — 17.6 x 25.0 cm

ISBN 92-826-5675-6

Price (excluding VAT) in Luxembourg: ECU 10